Creative Ideas for Decorating

Creative Ideas for Decorating

With the Editors of
CREATIVE IDEAS FOR LIVING®

Foreword by Katherine Pearson

Compiled & Edited by Julia Hamilton Thomason

Oxmoor House, Inc.
Birmingham

© 1987 by Oxmoor House, Inc.
Book Division of Southern Progress Corporation
P.O. Box 2463, Birmingham, Alabama 35201

Library of Congress Catalog Number: 85-52362
ISBN: 0-8487-0689-7
Manufactured in the United States of America

First Edition

Executive Editor: Candace N. Conard
Production Manager: Jerry Higdon
Associate Production Manager: Rick Litton
Art Director: Bob Nance

Creative Ideas for Decorating

Editor: Rebecca Morton Brennan
Designer: Cynthia R. Cooper
Editorial Assistant: Margaret Allen Northen
Production Assistant: Theresa L. Beste
Illustrator: Barbara Ball

Photographer & Designer credits appear on page 206.

Special thanks to Cynthia Rogers at *Creative Ideas for Living*
magazine for her invaluable assistance.

Contents

Foreword *9*

Introduction *12*

Color & Pattern *15*

    Plan a House Full of Color *16*
    Balance Cool & Warm Colors *21*
    Use Neutral Colors for an Elegant Richness *24*
    White as the Dominant Color *26*
    Unify with Color *30*
    Mix Patterns & Prints *32*
    Coordinate Paint & Fabric Colors *38*
    Dramatize with Rich Wall Colors *40*
    Focus on Stenciling *46*

Kitchens *51*

    Create a Welcoming Style *53*
    Flavor Contemporary Kitchens with Tradition *56*
    Warm the Kitchen with Crafts *59*
    Redecorate with Paint *62*
    Focus on Storage *64*

Dining Areas *67*

    Let Tables Set the Mood *69*
    Focus on the Table *74*
    Make Room for Entertaining *76*
    A Simply Elegant Dining Room *78*
    Expansive Ideas for a Small Area *81*

Living Spaces 85

A Light Look for a Country Room 86
A Change of Style 91
Creative Arrangements 95
Drama on a Small Stage 99
Create a Focal Point 101
Focus on the Fireplace 106
Storage from the Past 108
Choose the Right Area Rug 112
Accent with Soft Lighting 115
More than a Sunroom 116

Bedrooms 119

Master Bedroom Retreats 121
Create a Country French Look 126
Daybeds for Sitting & Sleeping 128
Fashion a Stylish Bedspread 131
Focus on Lace & Linens 132

Finishing Touches 135

Innovative Windows 136
Fancy Walls 140
Creative Displays 145
Tabletop Displays 150
Delicate Details 154

Creative Design 159

Walls 160

Hand-Painted Walls 160
    Combing 160
    Sponging 161
    Striating & Drybrushing 161
Stenciled Backsplash 163
Stenciled Walls 164

Windows 166

Window Shades 166
    Canvas Shade 166
    Tied Shade 167

No-Sew Window Treatments 168
Fabric Knot 168
Pouf Swag 169
Bow-Tied Swag 170
Easy-Sew Swag 171
Braided Edging 172

Floors 173

Painted Floors 173
Checkerboard Floor 173
Inlay Floor 173
Pickled Floor 174
Floorcoverings 175
Stenciled Floorcloth 175
Painted Sisal Rug 176
Fabric-Dyed Rug 177
Crocheted Rag Rug 178
Stenciled Rag Rug 178

Furniture 179

Hand-Painted Furniture 179
Faux Marble 179
Colorful Details 180
Milk Paint 182
Stenciled Furniture 184
Fabric-Dyed Furniture 186
Stenciling with Varnish 187
Light Wood Finishes 188
Pickling 188
Bleaching 188
Pierced-Tin Panels 190

Accessories 191

Tablecloths 191
Round Tablecloth 191
Round Tablecloth with Shirred Welt 192
Square or Rectangular Tablecloth 194
Simple Pillows 195
Tied Pillow Covers 195
Fancy Knotted Pillows 197
Painted Quilt-Block Pillows 198
Stylish Bedspreads 200
Bedspread from Sheets 200
Painted Damask Spread 201
Folding Screens 202
Painted Cutouts 204
Table Lamps 205

Photographer & Designer Credits 206

Index 212

Foreword

Perhaps the most important criteria for judging the merits of home decoration is how much a room tells you about the people who live there. Although the term is too often applied in a superficial way, personal style is indeed a measure of good design. Your home should say something about you—your interests, the region of the country where you live, your heritage, your talents, and your loves. In short, your home should look different from mine.

In the fast-paced, populous world that we live in today, the home becomes a rare place to express yourself. (It is that now whether you have planned it or not.) This uncharacteristic freedom is intimidating to the majority of homeowners who make the mistake of copying someone else's room or style exactly, rather than seeking out and expressing their own individuality.

This book does not dictate how you should live and decorate. Instead, it provides a strong foundation to help you make decorating decisions within any style that is most comfortable to you.

Current trends are apparent here. There is no doubt that keeping up with new trends is a pleasure, adding excitement to our lives and homes. But while trends will be replaced, the lessons within this book will still apply twenty-five years and three homes later. The most important investment you can make is to learn the basics of good design. You can then more easily sift through all of the popular looks, new directions, and overwhelming choices of furnishings available to you for the elements that you respond to most. And in doing so, you will instinctively define your own personal decorating style.

In addition to reflecting the people who live in them, all of the rooms on these pages have in common a welcoming, comfortable livability. When our Decorating Editor evaluates a home for a possible feature in *Creative Ideas for Living* magazine, one of her primary considerations is, Does it look like a family lives there? That same practical standard is upheld in this book.

For a room can reflect enormous style and sophistication in choices without being formal and grand. These pages are filled with good examples. Nothing warms and relaxes a room more than sharing personal things with friends who visit. Thus the rooms and lessons here are unintimidating—as your home should be.

In presenting the fundamentals of good decorating, we made a conscious decision not to limit ourselves (and you) to only one style of interiors. Our examples are drawn from all the livable decorating styles popular today. With the exception of a few people who have an innate sense of individual style, we have found that many homeowners like to enjoy several compatible looks within one house. It is not unusual to see formal eighteenth-century living and dining room furnishings with a contemporary kitchen, a country family room, and a romantic Victorian bedroom.

You will learn how to use the best of your country pieces and update them as this venerable style has evolved into lighter and often more romantic variations. English and French country rooms, the offshoots of American country, are well represented, too, with their relaxed sophistication, familiar clutter, and profusions of patterns. An outline of key elements and guidelines are provided to help you translate these continental country looks in your home.

More and more mothers have discovered that

comtemporary colors and materials are especially well suited to homes where there are growing children, and their decorating ideas are included. But it is contemporary with a difference—with a warmth that comes from an antique piece, a handmade quilt, and family collectibles. And from homes across America, we have gleaned the prettiest traditional furnishings, made fresh and decidedly unstuffy by the charm of the personal style.

All of the rooms you will see here are within reach, filled with ideas, projects, looks that you can easily adapt in your own decor. The country look remains popular in America's homes today because it looks achievable. Many women across the country have responded to this style with the feeling, That looks like something I could do! In this book (as we do in the magazine), we have taken the comforting do-ability quotient that makes country easy to pull together and applied it in simple lessons to make more sophisticated decorating styles just as accessible to you.

We have followed a few basic guidelines to what we call "good sense decorating." That is different from budget decorating, which is not necessarily a good idea. We are talking about a matter of balance, using your decorating dollars wisely to stretch them as far as possible.

Even the most celebrated interior designers have to toe the line when it comes to the budget. Regardless of how wealthy their clients seem to be, their resources—just like ours—are finite. And an interior designer can help you achieve a look you want at a price you can afford without ever hinting at compromise. We recommend that you pay for professional design advice where it is most helpful—in the selection of colors and fabric and furniture arrangement—and then do whatever work you can yourself.

Throughout the beautiful rooms shown here, we have highlighted specific projects that you can duplicate or adapt for your own home. (Look for complete instructions in the Creative Design chapter.) The surprise is that these do-it-yourself projects do not look it. The end results are polished and professional, belying the ease with which they can be accomplished. The benefits you will reap go beyond stretching the decorating budget; doing some of the work yourself guarantees that your personal expressions will come through in the finished room.

Other balancing acts, intended to keep you within your budget, can also pay off in achieving personal style. When making major purchases, for instance, such as upholstered seating, floor coverings, draperies, you should buy the best quality you can afford as these pieces will be with you for a long time. (Resist getting too trendy or dramatic in shape, color, and pattern, so that you *can* live with them for years.) If a wise purchase here uses up the lion's share of your budget, you can still pick up unusual secondary pieces for a song at antique shops, flea markets, and auctions. Rely on decorative painting to transform these modest pieces into fashionable accents.

Accessorize with family photographs, treasured books, houseplants, your own handwork, and favorite collections. Through these personal subjects your home reveals something of you and your family. It is here — in the simplest of ways — that a home becomes distinctly yours.

For all the enticing variety of rooms and decorating styles featured here, this book catalogs a particular viewpoint in decorating: the most successful interiors are those that reflect the owners. Our lessons are intended to make it easier for you to make the best decision regardless of what your particular preferences are. Our easy-to-do projects and instructions are included to help you put even more of yourself into your home.

Knowing that you — your own creativity and interests and history — are the essential element in successful interior design, use this book as a springboard to create a home that truly reflects your style.

Katherine Pearson

Editor, *Creative Ideas for Living*

11

Introduction

Welcome to the brightest and best ideas for decorating! Designer Julia Hamilton Thomason and the editors of *Creative Ideas for Decorating* magazine have combed the country for the most stunning, achievable decorating looks and techniques, and we present them to you here in one breathtaking volume.

Creative Ideas for Decorating is the key that will unlock your decorating imagination. With our focus on color, comfort, and originality, you will find dozens of ways to make your home more interesting and more inviting, without spending a fortune. We offer a portfolio of visual ideas, complete with instructions for specific projects and decorating techniques.

Successful decorating is as much an attitude as it is an activity, and *Creative Ideas for Decorating* will give you the confidence to bring personal style to your home with remarkable flair. The creative lessons in each of the chapters show you the special tricks of the trade, combining style and substance in a volume that is at once entertaining to read, yet also practical to use.

The book is composed of idea-packed chapters featuring living spaces, dining rooms, bedrooms, kitchens, and even finishing touches to add when the rest of the decorating is complete. Tips for working with color, pattern, fabric, and furniture abound in the vivid color photographs. And every photograph contains at least one, often several, innovative and practical solutions for overcoming common obstacles to successful decorating. The

large, inviting format will inspire you with creative ideas for every room in your house.

Notations under many of the photographs throughout the book refer you to instructions in the Creative Design chapter. You will turn to this chapter often for its easy-to-follow instructions for creating many of the delightful accents you saw in the earlier chapters, plus a few surprises.

The Creative Design chapter provides a rich source for adding your own distinctively individual ambience to your home. Here, we have avoided giving instructions for the more obvious decorating styles and have chosen instead to assemble a wealth of unique decorating ideas and innovative creative design projects, some of which require a few basic craft skills, such as sewing or painting. Every area of your house will gain new importance with the addition of something handmade or hand painted, whether it is a stenciled border for a rug, a braided edging on draperies, or a hand-painted pedestal for a dining table.

There are so many ways to use the practical ideas shown throughout *Creative Ideas for Decorating.* Rather than trying to duplicate exactly what is shown in this book, you may sometimes choose to use our techniques as a springboard for your own more personal decorating ideas. Just keep in mind that as you furnish and decorate your home, allow for future changes that will reflect your family's varying activities and developing interests.

You might use current fashion to give your

12

home a new look. Often just a splash of color or fabric is all that is needed to bring a room up-to-date. Do not hesitate to substitute a readily available material for something that is expensive or difficult to find.

If you are short on artwork or accessories to make a room unique, improvise by using a familiar object in a new way. For example, a large seashell makes a perfect soap dish. Even a clay pot can have new life as a charming lamp for a kitchen. (We tell you how easy it is to make a lamp in our Creative Design chapter.) With a little effort and perhaps a bit of sewing or stenciling, you can transform an attic treasure or a flea-market find into an heirloom. A great way to obtain unusual accessories is to purchase decorative objects and then personalize them in some way. For example, a plain paper shade on a brass or porcelain lamp could be easily painted or stenciled, using the instructions in this book. Even the most carefully furnished traditional room will gain new character with such an understated accent.

As you approach any decorating project, remember that the way a house lives is far more important than the way it looks. A comfortable, enjoyable home, rather than a specific visual effect, should be the ultimate goal of any successful decorating plan.

Color & Pattern

The creative blending of colors and patterns can enliven or calm a room, create a focal point, or cover a flaw. A delicious new paint color and a touch of elegantly patterned fabric can change the character of a room and perhaps even set the mood for your entire house.

Plan a House Full of Color

Creating a logical flow of color through several rooms in a house may be much easier than you think. Start by choosing one key color, then expand it into a color scheme for the entire house.

You might begin by selecting a wallpaper that features your color choice along with several other hues that can be used in planning the wall, fabric, and accessory colors for the house. Colors taken from the wallpaper can be featured, of course, on walls, but they can also provide the inspiration for innovative combinations on wood trims, windows, even bathroom tiles. The color scheme for the whole house can revolve around your favorite colors featured in just one wallpaper design.

To avoid using the same color in each room of the house, yet still enjoy a related color scheme, a central hallway can serve as the transition space from one colorful area to the next. Paper the

▼ *Wallpaper in a central hallway eases the transition from one colorful room to the next. The pink, aqua, yellow, peach, and blue in the wallpaper provides the inspiration for wall, fabric, and accessory colors in the other rooms.*

▲ *Pink walls make a contemporary foil for traditional dining room furniture. Walls below the chair rail are covered with the same striped paper used in the hallway.*

hallway with your choice of wallpaper, then paint each room a different color contained in the paper for a versatile, creatively coordinated personal color scheme.

Using wallpaper as the basis for your color selection is only one way to plan the color for your house. Consider incorporating the wall colors from several different rooms in a stenciled border. Stencil the border around a doorway to frame the view of a colorful room and perhaps repeat the border on the wall in an adjoining room to unify the different colors.

Fabric is another ideal source of inspiration for finding colors that work well together. Take the fabric used for slipcovers in one room and use that same fabric to skirt a table, line draperies, or cover accent pillows in nearby rooms.

◄ *In the sunroom, a mix of patterns in soft pastels echoes the colors of the hallway paper and creates a restful mood for reading and relaxing. Shelves constructed around the window create an architectural framework for the daybed.*

▲ *Pale aqua and jet black make a dramatic combination in a small bathroom. A wallpaper border adds rich color and just the right touch of pattern.*

▲ *Serene blue walls in the bedroom accentuate the warm color of the stripped pine furniture.*

Balance Cool & Warm Colors

You can use a number of different colors in a room as long as they are well balanced. The way to add a spark of interest and still have a harmonious color scheme is to play warm colors against cool colors. Adding a touch of warm color is a subtle way to enliven a room that is predominantly cool in tone. In much the same way, accent pieces in cool colors will enrich and complement the warm tones in a room.

Warm colors contain reds, yellows, and oranges and include hues such as pumpkin, buttercup, shrimp, saffron, peach, and pink. Warm colors appear to advance visually. They seem to fill space, making a large room seem smaller, more cozy.

Cool colors, such as lavender, mint, and sage, contain blues, greens, and violets and appear to recede. Because they are light in value, cool colors give even small areas a feeling of spaciousness.

To create a restful mood in a room, limit bright, warm colors to small items, such as pillows, accessories, or small chairs. Use cool or neutral tones for large areas, such as walls, floor, ceiling, and big pieces of furniture.

◄ *Walls in a sunny living room are painted a warm pumpkin color. The cool greens and blues of the furniture look comfortable and welcoming when balanced with the mellow wall color.*

▼ *The cool blues and violets in the madras tablecloth, rug, and checked curtains enliven the color scheme in the breakfast area. The use of the same pumpkin wall color repeats the warm feeling of the adjoining living room.*

►In a small cottage living room, gray walls make a cool background for a warm peach sofa. The dhurrie rug containing both cool and warm colors helps tie the scheme together. An antique French rabbit coop, covered with glass, works well as an interesting—and airy—coffee table.

▲ The living room's cool and warm tones are echoed again in the skirted end table, which cleverly conceals large stereo speakers. (Instructions for making a round tablecloth are in the Creative Design chapter.)

▲ *The neutral wall color, pulled from a shade in the Oriental rug, makes an understated backdrop for fine art and furniture.*

Use Neutral Colors for an Elegant Richness

Lush neutral colors have a richness that enables you to create quietly elegant rooms without using a lot of color. You can achieve a neutral look by building a color scheme around a favorite sofa, chair, rug, or painting. Let the color and character of that one piece suggest ways to handle the rest of the room.

For example, choose a wall color that duplicates one of the lightest neutral shades in a favorite rug. Accent colors can also be pulled from the rug to use in upholstery fabrics and accessories.

Using the same color for the ceiling and walls, or a color that is a few shades lighter or darker, further enhances a monochromatic scheme and lends continuity to spaces—an especially desirable effect in odd-shaped rooms. Similar neutral tones on the ceiling, floor, and walls also work well to make narrow rooms appear larger and less crowded. White crown molding helps to pull the eye upward, adding to a room's perceived height.

Large pieces of furniture contribute an important element in a neutral room. A sofa in a timeless style and neutral color, such as cream, white, or gray, is one of the most versatile purchases you will ever make. With a quick change of pillows and accessories, you will be able to use it in any setting, with any color scheme.

▼ *The intricately patterned rug also provides the palette for accent colors in the room. Pillows made from fragments of old rugs add additional interesting patterns.*

▲ *A simply elegant window treatment combines a neutral fabric shade with gathered draperies for a classic look. The room's monochromatic color scheme is successfully carried out through the use of the same neutral tone in the major elements of the room—the draperies, window shade, wall color, and rug.*

24

▲ Neutral tones in a bedroom create a quiet, refined environment. Draperies raised to the ceiling add to the room's perceived height.

◄ A richly colored rug adds an intriguing splash of color to a bedside table. Colors become even more dramatic when placed against a background of neutrals.

White as the Dominant Color

A white color scheme might seem to be the ultimate challenge in decorating, but a limited palette actually offers a variety of interesting design options.

One good approach is to capitalize on texture by mixing rough and smooth surfaces in a room. Cushions of fine, white linen, for example, create an unexpected, yet pleasing contrast to a rustic wooden chair. An all-white quilt hung behind a bleached oak table makes an excellent backdrop for natural objects, such as a shell collection or a piece of driftwood. A white room even enhances baskets and wicker by accentuating their textures.

By removing color, the subtle details of a room are emphasized, making shapes and shadows, such as those in canvas draperies or crown molding, appear more important. Fine details in a lace pillow or a crocheted canopy gain more notice when they are not competing with a strong color.

Even wood takes on new importance in an all-white room, especially blond wood such as birch, white pine, and oak. Offering balance and warmth, the natural color of wood acts as a foil for a white wall color.

Initially, white surroundings might seem to be too pristine to be both livable and interesting, but by varying materials and the way they are used, you can achieve a variety of different environments throughout the house. In the bathroom, for example, combine sparkling white porcelain with shiny tile or marble for added gleam. Use soft textiles such as a white cotton rug or thick, white towels to contrast with the more durable surfaces of the room. In the kitchen, white surfaces maximize the feeling of space, especially in a small area.

White can evoke a true sense of refinement in a formal setting. A creamy damask or white-on-white brocade upholstery is especially effective when complemented with elegant silver and crystal accessories.

The use of white can even help to unify otherwise diverse elements. Architectural features such

► *The sleek, contemporary look of a predominantly white living room is enhanced by the use of bold accent colors.*

as a cathedral ceiling, rock fireplace, and built-in storage area might compete visually when used in the same room, diminishing the impact of each individual feature. Painting all of the different features in the room white, including the walls and ceiling, helps to unify them and creates a pleasing neutral background for adding bright color in the furnishings.

▼ *Pearly white walls, wicker, and crisp bed linens create a mood of repose and relaxation in a guest room. The quilt adds a quiet note of pattern and color.*

◄ *When wood is used architecturally, a white ceiling and walls accent its color and grain. White also makes an excellent neutral backdrop for displaying art.*

▼ *Pristine white cabinets and countertops give a small kitchen the illusion of spaciousness.*

▲ *White paint unifies the distinctive architectural features in a large family room. The white cathedral ceiling, rock fireplace, and shuttered storage wall work together to provide an open, airy ambience.*

◄ *Simple canvas shades require a minimum of fabric, yet provide full control of light and privacy. Their white color contributes to the room's spacious look. (Instructions for making fabric shades are in the Creative Design chapter.)*

Unify with Color

Most people acquire furniture over a lifetime by purchasing some things and inheriting others. The result can be an interesting mix of pieces that may be unmatched in the usual sense. Such a collection is a good basis for creating a truly individual look.

Color is your best ally in unifying furniture styles. By having sofas and chairs upholstered in the same fabric, you can combine unrelated pieces and create the look of a coordinated furniture grouping. The unifying fabric color makes differences in shapes and contours of the furniture become less evident.

Several pieces of furniture covered in the same rich color of fabric can also provide a focus of deep color for a room. Wood surfaces of similar tones will unify the look of disparate objects, as well.

▼ *The fabric used to upholster the chairs and cover the cushions in a family room updates and unifies the vintage wood pieces.*

▲ *Large surfaces in the den, such as the walls, floor, sofa, and chair, are solid colors; while smaller chairs, accessories, and paintings bring in more color and pattern. Hunter green upholstery fabric draws the sofa, chair, and ottoman together and provides a focus of color for the room.*

Mix Patterns & Prints

Fabric is one of the most important elements in creating the right mood for a room. A large, open room becomes cozy with bold, colorful fabrics. A small room can be made to appear more roomy by using fabrics in soft shades and pastels. In either case, mixing prints and patterns provides you with a whole new realm of decorating possibilities.

Color and proportion are extremely important, and often trial and error is the only way to see whether a combination will work. Manufacturer coordinated fabrics eliminate a lot of the guesswork when putting together a roomful of mixed prints, but with a few guidelines, you can easily combine prints and patterns to suit your own individual taste.

Mix the patterns with care. Use only one bold pattern in a room and use it on a broad surface, where it really stands out. Secondary prints should vary in size, but everything should be smaller in scale than the primary print.

Match the rhythm of the patterns. Patterns with angular lines look best with straight-sided furniture. Design motifs with rounded edges, such as dots and flowers, are more suited to furniture with soft curves.

Analyze the way prints work with each other. Small allover prints lose a lot of detail from a distance and almost resemble solid fabrics. Plaids and checks, on the other hand, add the spark of contrasting colors and perhaps are best reserved for accent pieces.

▶ *Bold colors and patterns make a large family room appear more cozy. The large graphic design used on the overstuffed chairs works well with the single-color checked fabric used on other pieces.*

▲ *Bright checks on the chair seats and on the French doors add to the dining area's comfortable look and help pull the decorating scheme from the living room into the other rooms of the house.*

▲ *The same cheerful checked fabric is used on the cornice at the kitchen window and coordinates well with the adjoining dining area and family room.*

▲ *The bold flowered pattern used on a sofa and chair is accented with more subtle secondary prints.*

◄ *The patterns and prints in the chair, wallpaper, and window treatment blend with ease. The bold fabric of the accent pillows is complemented by the smaller design used on the other elements. Similar shades of blue and rose strengthen the fabric mix.*

▼ *The creatively coordinated fabrics of the rose-patterned sofa, the fabric-covered sofa table, and the plaid laminated tray demonstrate a successful mix of prints and patterns.*

Coordinate Paint & Fabric Colors

Whether you are painting porch furniture or bedroom walls, there is a foolproof way to find just the right color and shade of paint to coordinate with your fabrics.

To select the shade of paint that works best with the fabrics you have chosen, use graduated chips of color from a paint store. These paint chips typically show a progression of several shades of a single color, ranging from light to dark. The color chips can provide a helpful guideline for coordinating a color scheme.

To find the best light shade to use with a dark fabric, simply select a color chip that matches your fabric color. Then choose the lightest tint on the card to paint the walls or furniture.

Reverse the procedure to find the best dark shade of paint to use with a light fabric. Match your light fabric to a paint chip. Then use the darkest shade on the card for painting.

▶ *Dark green towels were selected for covering the chair cushions on wicker furniture. The color for the furniture was determined by finding the lightest tint on a paint card whose darkest tint matched the green towels. A flowered sheet was chosen for accessory pieces since it repeats the green of the chair cushions and adds pink as an accent color. Solid-color sheets were also used to cover pillows and to make a crocheted rug. (Instructions for making a crocheted rag rug and a round tablecloth are in the Creative Design chapter.)*

▲ *Accent pillows covered in a mixture of coordinating solids and prints add a pleasant contrast to the dark green cushions. A side chair painted in a pastel tone reinforces the accent color.*

Dramatize with Rich Wall Colors

Dark colors add depth and richness to a wide range of decorating styles. Depending on the shade you choose, deep color can create a sense of tranquility in a bedroom, for instance, or a hint of drama in a dining room. At night, walls painted with colors such as hunter green, cranberry, terracotta, or burgundy appear to recede and can make a room look larger. By day, natural light seems even brighter in contrast to a dark wall color.

Dark walls can dramatize moldings, fireplaces, and windows. You can then focus attention on unique architectural details by painting them white. For a touch of pattern, use borders of stenciled designs along the moldings. To disguise awkward architectural elements, paint walls and woodwork the same dark color.

A variety of decorating moods can be enhanced by rich wall colors. In summer, use accessories

sparingly to create a cool, open feeling. Change to white slipcovers for a crisp contrast to the dark walls. In winter, replace the white with earth-toned pieces for a warm feeling. Darker slipcovers and quilts can also help to change the mood.

If you are afraid that a deep wall color will make a room seem too somber, keep the floors light, use white or natural draperies, or hang a mirror on one wall to expand the room.

One of the most difficult aspects of changing to a dark wall color is finding the right shade. Having a fabric or accessory, such as a bedspread or quilt, to build around makes it easier. Paint several test areas on a wall; then choose the one that matches the fabric most closely.

Pale wood, whether in furniture, woodwork, or accessories, offers another approach to balancing dark walls. The subtle golden warmth of pine, oak, and birch seems to glow in contrast to the deep wall color. Hanging a colorful quilt or needlework, adding baskets, grapevine wreaths, or other accent pieces capitalizes on the wall color as a dramatic background.

◄ *A deep hunter green wall brings out the brilliant colors of the patchwork quilt in a living room. Window frames were painted the same color as the wall to disguise awkward window spacing.*

▲ *White moldings stand out in sharp contrast against warm brown walls. Stenciling in red, white, and yellow adds a quaint touch of pattern. (Instructions for stenciling are in the Creative Design chapter.)*

◄ *Each of four shutter panels was sawed from a solid piece of wood to fit within the window frame. The shutters were first given a light coat of stain to echo the brown tones of the walls and then stenciled.*

(Overleaf) A rich aqua wall color emphasizes the crisp, white woodwork, bookshelves, and fireplace in an elegant living room.

◄ *The raspberry walls of the dining room are beautifully enriched by the pale wood tones of the table and chairs. (Instructions for painting a sisal rug are in the Creative Design chapter.)*

Classic, white woodwork balances dark matte-finish walls and oak floors, creating an airy, out-of-doors ...ing. The color of the wall closely matches the green of the rose leaves on the comforter.

Focus on Stenciling

Stenciling is an expressive way to add a personal touch to your room, whether it is country, traditional, or contemporary. The simplest way to coordinate a stencil pattern with room furnishings is to take the pattern from fabric or wallpaper used in the room. Using stencils of similar patterns smooths the transition from one room into an adjoining room, and the similar colors from the fabric and wallpaper help to unify the stenciled room. Start with a basic stencil pattern; then use your imagination for surprisingly fresh ideas for stenciling. Instructions for stenciling are in the Creative Design chapter.

▲ *Stenciling need not be limited to borders. A casual floral design adds a lovely accent.*

▲ *The leaf pattern stenciled along a chair rail echoes the pattern and color of the pillow fabric.*

▲ *The style, size, and color of a stencil design were tailored to fit the backsplash area of a kitchen counter. (Instructions and the pattern for a stenciled backsplash are in the Creative Design chapter.)*

▲ *A delicate scroll stencil is complemented by the distinctive colors of an intricately detailed molding.*

47

▲ A delicate flowering vine trails only a short distance on the center molding of a double window.

▼ Stenciled tulips and polka dots brighten the walls of a little girl's room. The background grid of dots was marked with a pencil and then painted. The room was visually scaled down by stenciling the generous space above the molding with a large flower spray designed to go with the comforter and wallpaper motifs.

▲ The large scale of the parading geese makes them a focal point for a child's room, while creating the illusion of a cozier, smaller room. Although it looks as though there are many different geese, only four stencil designs were applied in a random sequence. The ribbon was painted on freehand.

▶ The goose motif may be repeated on a rag rug in an adjoining bathroom. Contrasting grosgrain ribbon bows add texture and color to the geese without more painting.

48

◄ *Random placement of motifs and a few changes in scale and detail keep a stencil design from looking repetitious. A simple piece of canvas was transformed into a whimsical floor cloth, an antique church pew was enlivened with an ivy border, while frolicking sheep and a border of flowers add a distinctive look to a blanket chest.*

▼ *Stenciled bows and baskets are key components in a charming country French kitchen. The kitchen fireplace is brightened in warm months by a fire screen stenciled to match the cabinets. The screen is a sheet of painted plywood with shelf brackets attached to form the stand.*

▲ *A little stenciling will rejuvenate an old piece of furniture. Botanical prints make lovely stenciling patterns.*

49

Kitchens

Everyone loves the warmth of an inviting kitchen. Add decorative flair to even the most compact space with touches of your own crafts or by using a special antique for storage and display.

▲ *Brick is the unifying element in an elegant kitchen and family room. The brick fireplace, floor, and kitchen wall serve to unify the rooms and give the two areas a warm, cozy atmosphere.*

Create a
Welcoming Style

A big family kitchen with a large table, an easy chair, and a feeling of space is the ideal arrangement for many homeowners. However, you may be the kind of cook who likes a compact working area. If you prefer a small and efficient galley to a more spacious kitchen, you can arrange the kitchen to provide both a compact working area for serious cooking and a welcoming environment for family and friends.

Start with a small kitchen, organize it efficiently, and then open it up to a nearby family room. The kitchen is convenient for cooking, since all appliances are within easy reach, and the cook can still enjoy being a part of the family room activities. An island or counter between the kitchen and family room provides a graceful, as well as functional transition between the two areas. On the family room side, you might extend the countertop a foot or so to provide a place for stools for extra seating. Add favorite elements, such as books, artwork, and plants, to the kitchen area for a visual transition, and it becomes one of the most comfortable and inviting places in your entire house.

▲ Books, plants, and comfortable chairs create an inviting sitting area in a kitchen and family room combination.

◄ An island countertop provides space for eating and working and is a graceful transition between the two areas. The open shelves overhead add storage space and contribute to the open feeling of the room.

▶ *A wall was removed from one side of the kitchen to open up the space to the family room addition. Brick-patterned flooring and an area rug such as the ones used in the family room help to unite the kitchen and seating area.*

▲ *Area rugs overlap casually in front of comfortable wing chairs and add color and pattern to the room. A pewter and oak baker's rack makes an excellent display case for a creative mix of plants and collectibles.*

◄ *One side of the kitchen island houses a television set; a sink and kitchen storage area are included on the opposite side, which is slightly higher to help separate the two functions.*

Flavor Contemporary Kitchens with Tradition

Designers often use a single piece of contemporary furniture, such as an acrylic coffee table or a modern sofa, as an accent in a room of antiques, knowing that a mix of furniture from different periods makes an effective contrast of styles.

If you like the efficiency and clean appearance of contemporary kitchen cabinets, yet prefer traditional furniture for the rest of the house, you can easily combine the best of both styles in the kitchen. Use your contemporary kitchen as a background for a special piece of antique or reproduction furniture. Traditional furniture adds pleasant warmth and charm to contemporary settings, while providing extra storage or seating space.

▲ *The ambience of the small breakfast area reflects the traditional flavor of the furnishings in the rest of the house.*

▲ *The Oriental floor runner bridges the transition from sleek, contemporary kitchen to the more traditional dining area. A soft almond color on the cabinets, walls, and floor affords the flexibility of changing the look of the room by simply changing the floor runner, table linens, and draperies.*

◄ *The breakfast area softens the lines of the kitchen with a buttermilk-painted jam cupboard and a farmhouse table, each authentic American antiques.*

▼ *A serene style permeates a fairly contemporary kitchen thanks to a mix of antique and reproduction furniture set against a background of new cabinetwork.*

58

Warm the Kitchen with Crafts

A well-designed kitchen filled with new appliances and cookware can be a joy to use. But for all their efficiency and performance, too many of these modern tools can make a kitchen seem a bit over-mechanized.

To bring back warmth without sacrificing practicality, look to your collections of artwork and handcrafts to find new accessories for the kitchen. With a bit of creative display, you can easily balance the technology of the kitchen with a touch of your personal style.

Add a splash of color and texture by hanging a special painting or a favorite quilt on a wall. In a room filled with identical cabinets, a large quilt or framed print creates a much-needed focal point. Use hooks to hang a basket collection from a pot rack or ceiling beam.

If the tops of your wall cabinets are accessible, use these areas to display baskets, old tins, and other collectibles. Place a small light among the objects for added drama at night. Kitchen shelves are ideal for creative arrangements of folk art and crafts. Vary the collection from time to time, just as you would change accessories in any other room of the house.

The thoughtful placement of your own special treasures will transform a utilitarian kitchen into a cozy spot for both family and guests.

◄ *An Amish quilt and two antique cabinets warm an otherwise all-white kitchen. Open kitchen shelves make an excellent display area for favorite collectibles.*

▲ *A large painting placed at one end of a kitchen adds an accent of contrasting color to the room.*

▲ *Pottery and linen toweling turn an unused pantry corner into a quiet retreat. Spray adhesive makes covering the walls and desk pad with fabric easy.*

▲ *Whimsical place mats, homemade jellies and jams attractively displayed, and a scattering of handcrafted treasures add a warm, personal touch to a bright, fresh kitchen.*

▲ *Pristine white cabinets and walls provide a perfect backdrop for the display of brightly colored pieces of folk art.*

◄ *Touches of quilting accent a breakfast table and an old cherry sofa. Quilt-block pillows can be sewn using almost any quilt pattern, or the designs can be painted on fabric. (Instructions for painting a quilt-block pillow are in the Creative Design chapter.)*

▲ *A colorful mix of collectibles and kitchen tools enlivens a corner with decorative flair.*

Redecorate with Paint

Painting is the most practical and inexpensive way to freshen and brighten your kitchen. Simply painting walls and woodwork can create a whole new look. You can paint cabinets, floors, even appliances, and paint can also be used to emphasize the wood trim around doors and windows. Touches of decorative stenciling can add a lively pattern, as well as help to unify the room's colors.

Painting Cabinets

It is not always necessary to strip wood cabinets before painting. However, paint may chip in time; therefore, it is essential that you prepare the wood so that the paint will adhere well.

The first steps in painting cabinets are to remove all the cabinet hardware, take the doors off the cabinet frame, and remove all drawers. Then scrub the wood surfaces with a heavy-duty liquid cleaner or detergent. Allow the surface to dry thoroughly and sand lightly.

Professional painters recommend using an oil-base primer, although for the second coat you can use either oil or latex paint. A high-gloss paint is a good choice for kitchen cabinets, since a shiny surface looks fresh and will be easier to keep clean than a surface painted with flat paint.

Appliance Colors

You do not have to replace old appliances that are still in good working order to update a kitchen's look. To de-emphasize the appliance color, consider a light, neutral color for the overall kitchen. Floors, walls, countertops, and cabinets are big surface areas that will work well in a neutral background color. Or try fashionable accent colors that will draw attention away from the older appliance colors. Fresh colors can be introduced in window treatments, table settings, wallpaper, stenciling, painted trim, and accessories.

Appliances can be professionally repainted. Check the yellow pages under "appliances" for repainting services or ask for recommendations at interior decorating shops. Appliance manufacturers usually do not recommend repainting since the second finish is often not as durable as the original, but on older appliances you may find repainting to be a satisfactory temporary solution. Refrigerators and dishwashers can usually be repainted with good results. However, appliances that give off high heat, such as ovens and cooking tops, are more difficult to paint, since the high temperatures eventually can cause the paint to peel.

▲ *Paint adds color and creates a look of true individuality in a casual kitchen. Open wall cabinets and moldings were painted brick red. Base cabinets are brick red with green doors. Touches of stenciling add a quaint touch of pattern to the white wood-plank walls. (Instructions for stenciling walls are in the Creative Design chapter.)*

▲ *The lower cabinets of a kitchen were updated with a coat of soft blue-green paint. The surface of the dishwasher was scuffed with steel wool, then painted with the same blue-green color in an oil-base enamel for a coordinated look.*

▲ *A small kitchen was visually enlarged by painting the cabinets, table, and chairs a fresh, sparkling white. To carry out the kitchen's blue-and-white theme, the floor was painted in a blue-and-white checkerboard pattern. (Instructions for painting a checkerboard floor are in the Creative Design chapter.)*

▲ *The look of old glass cabinet doors was recreated with standard window sashes, which are cheaper than custom-made mullioned doors. The frosted glass camouflages the basic necessities stored within.*

Focus on Storage

The creative design and placement of cabinets, open shelves, and built-in storage areas in your kitchen can be one of the most important decorative statements in the entire room. A glass-front cabinet, a bit of shelving, or an open compartment constructed between cabinets add architectural interest to this most functional of rooms, while allowing you the luxury of additional space to display your prettiest cookware and your favorite collectibles.

▲ *Adding a glass-paned door to a pantry cleverly transforms it into an attractive china closet. Silver and crystal are beautifully displayed under overhead lighting.*

▲ *Pierced-tin panels add a unique creative element to kitchen cabinets. (Instructions for making pierced-tin panels are in the Creative Design chapter.)*

▲ Simple arched frames on glass-front cabinets evoke a cozy, European ambience.

▲ Glass-front cabinets and open shelving provide abundant storage and display space. Glass doors give a lighter look to base cabinets below the tile work surface.

▲ An antique cabinet provides space for the storage and display of favorite pieces of china, while adding the warm glow of wood to a traditional kitchen.

Dining Areas

The dining room is the setting for many special occasions—festive holiday dinners, elegant receptions, intimate candlelight suppers. Create a uniquely personal ambience with out-of-the-ordinary table settings and imaginative room arrangements.

Let Tables Set the Mood

Decorating a dining room is different from decorating any other room in the house. Because this room is used frequently for entertaining, the style here can be much more dramatic than the rest of your home.

Much of the dining room is dominated by wooden pieces, such as the table, chairs, and buffet, so the decorating challenge is to soften the mood of the room and determine its theme without adding unnecessary furniture. The dining table, usually the largest single piece of furniture in the room, can easily set the mood for the entire area.

If your dining table is too small, you can expand it by placing a larger circle of wood over it. Add a round, floor-length tablecloth, and you have a new look for your room. Not only does the new, larger table change the personality of the dining area, but you can quickly go from a formal look to a casual one by simply changing the tablecloth.

A simple antique table combined with several comfortable chairs can give your whole room a cozy ambience. With just a few accessories, perhaps a primitive painting or some handmade pottery, you can create a look that is truly your own.

Use the top of your dining table to enhance the room's mood. Instead of the conventional large centerpiece for the table, arrange a row of different-shaped bud vases down the center of the table. Or use large pots of seasonal flowers on your table, such as geraniums and impatiens in the spring, for a fresh change. A few of your special collectibles, attractively arranged, also make a unique, very personal year-round table decoration.

◀ *A simple plywood circle covered with a wonderful round cloth turns any base into a dining room table. Change the cloth to change the mood. For a romantic look in the evening, scatter strings of tiny, white Christmas lights among the leaves of a large potted plant. (Instructions for making a round tablecloth are in the Creative Design chapter.)*

◄ *Long benches are interesting alternatives to chairs when used with a somewhat primitive dining table.*

▲ *An antique table echoes the homespun look of the tongue-and-groove ceiling and wood-plank walls in the dining room. Using pieces with similar wood tones enhances the unity of the grouping.*

▲ *Using a pedestal and adding a glass tabletop is an economical way to create a dramatic look. Pedestals can be as simple as a pair of wooden boxes painted to resemble marble. (Instructions for painting a faux finish are in the Creative Design chapter.)*

◄ *Bent willow chairs, quite different from the usual dining room furniture, set a very unique and unexpected mood in a dining area. A glass-topped table reinforces the open, airy look of the room.*

▼ *A table with a glass top and glass base allows the dining room to assume any mood. Dining chairs and accent pieces become the key elements in setting the decorating scheme.*

Focus on the Table

Your tabletop can set the mood — any mood — for dining. Venture out of the dining room for decorative items that will add an innovative spark of creativity to your table settings. The easiest way to change a table setting is by mixing styles. Baskets, pottery, porcelain bowls, statuary, houseplants, crystal candy dishes, and small bottles are just a sampling of the objects you probably have on hand that can help set a very special table with a variety of different moods.

▲ *Lace-and-linen place mats, turned sideways for a different effect, soften a wooden table.*

▲ *Even an informal banquette can be dressed up for a special occasion. The dark surface of the antique table showcases the intricate detail of heirloom needlework. Delicate crocheted doilies on colored plates make beautiful serving pieces, while adding to the formal look of the table. The doilies are protected by clear glass plates.*

▲ For the feeling of a picnic indoors, shallow baskets and crisp, plaid napkins relax the formality of a traditional dining room. A large basket holding cyclamen serves as a colorful centerpiece, while complementing the casual table setting.

▲ A tiny tabletop makes an intimate dining spot for a single setting. Hand towels, normally reserved for the kitchen, gain new prominence under delicate china.

▲ Pottery and handwoven mats are a casual contrast to a formal dining room setting. The rough texture of the fabric mats adds warmth to the smooth surface of the glass table.

Make Room
for Entertaining

A large formal living room with an adjoining smaller dining room is a fairly standard architectural arrangement, and it usually works well for most families. If, however, you find that you need more room for entertaining in the dining room, you might consider a switch.

In many houses, you need only to exchange furnishings in the two rooms to make a successful

rearrangement. If a chandelier has to be removed from the former dining room, simply cap the opening and paint it the same color as the ceiling. The use of similar wall colors in both rooms provides a harmonious flow from one area into the other. Similar accent colors in pillows, chair cushions, and accessories will also unify the two rooms.

A major consideration in making this kind of transition is the size of the furniture. Be sure that the scale of your dining furniture suits the larger room and the scale and number of living room pieces fit well into the smaller room.

◄ A spacious dining room and cozy living room were once reversed. But the dining room was too small for entertaining, and the living room was rarely used. Switching the furniture was a practical solution.

▼ Because of the small amount of space, the living room was furnished with two small love seats. Neutral colors help make the room appear larger than it really is.

A Simply Elegant Dining Room

The country look is one of the most comfortable, easy-living decorating styles. However, with just a few changes you can update a country look to make it a bit softer, more elegant.

The pine cupboard, an anchor in a country-look dining room, is a good place to begin your transition. Replace blue-and-white spackled enamelware, rustic cookware, and small country collectibles with china in a pretty fruit or floral pattern. Add antique linens and a few pieces of pewter for a delicate display.

Your choice of dining chairs can also make a noticeable difference in updating a country look. Replacing old, ladder-back chairs with a more refined, curved style will dress up the dining room, adding a gentle touch to the decor. Or transform your ladder-back chairs with the addition of seat and back cushions made from fabric with a small print background and tied on with pretty bows.

Instead of the typical cafe curtains and ruffled muslin tiebacks, you might want to try a simple swag window treatment. A swag works well with existing shutters or with antique linens shirred on a tension rod. Teamed in this way with other methods for controlling light and privacy, the swag requires much less fabric than a working shade and adds a fresh, updated look to the window.

▼ *Pine cupboards are appropriate to any country style of decorating, but delicate china plates and pewter pieces update the look.*

▲ *Rich green walls are a dramatic background for country pine cabinets and peach accents. Gently curved chairs, the elegant peach swag, and a graceful chandelier update this country look. (Instructions for making the swag are in the Creative Design chapter.)*

Expansive Ideas for a Small Area

A small dining room is a challenge to decorate, because you need to provide serving, seating, and table space all in the same area. However, with a little planning, you can furnish a small space with great flair and efficiency.

A glass tabletop is ideal for making a small room appear larger. A glass-topped table is elegant, classic, and usually compatible with a variety of furnishings. The transparent tabletop seems to take up less area than a wooden table, thus creating an illusion of more space. For a substantial-looking tabletop, the glass should be at least three-fourths of an inch thick. A beveled or rounded edge helps protect against chips.

The base of a glass-topped table sets its style. Select an exotic, fanciful base for a sophisticated look. Choose a cylinder of polished steel, and the effect is sleek and modern. Use reproductions of fluted columns or a Chippendale base to blend with traditional furniture.

If there is no space for a small buffet in your dining area, you can achieve the same result with a narrow wall-mounted shelf. A shelf placed conveniently by the dining table can hold candles, flowers, and other small items you may need during the course of a meal, such as cream and sugar or cruets for oil and vinegar. The shelf can be made of either glass or wood. For support, use attractive brackets attached securely to wall studs.

Fabric shades are a good window treatment for a small room, since they are not as space consuming as draperies. A neutral-color fabric for the shade will also add to the spacious feeling of the room.

▲ *A narrow glass shelf mounted on decorative wall brackets makes an attractive, space-saving server.*

◄ *A glass-topped table and wall shelf provide necessary surface area while visually enlarging a small dining room. The elegant dolphin pedestal adds a sophisticated touch. Fabric shades in a neutral color are perfect for a small area. (Instructions for making fabric shades are in the Creative Design chapter.)*

▲ A mellow pine storage box abloom with begonias enlivens a small serving area. A glass top, resting on old wrought iron brackets, holds a silver tray with decanters, a mahogany box, and ornate silver candlesticks. The pine box balances the oil painting above.

▶ A pine bench placed against one wall provides necessary seating without using a lot of space. A lighthearted mix of pine furniture is complemented by a soft rose tint in fabrics, rag rug, china, and flowers. A wall-hung corner cabinet and a rustic folk art painting successfully balance the height and visual weight of the pine cupboard opposite the bench. For a whimsical touch, a bird's nest is placed in the ficus.

Living Spaces

The living spaces of a house are where we entertain friends, enjoy our families, relax, and reflect. Consider the selection and arrangement of furniture, the availability of storage, and the use of lighting to create a welcoming, comfortable environment.

A Light Look for a Country Room

If you like the look of country but not all the clutter, you can lighten the look and still retain the cozy mood by using pastel colors, pale wood finishes, and just a few key accessories. Combine new furniture and antiques to create a fresh country ambience, then accessorize with a few homemade pieces and a little creativity. Decorating even a large room in this variation on a country theme can be relatively inexpensive.

Use your own crafts, such as quilt-block pillows and painted baskets, as accessories. Twisted-vine wreaths, seashells from your vacation, or any natural object can blend beautifully with antique quilts, handmade pottery, even modern woven rugs for a unique, personal design.

Instead of relying solely on antiques or purchased furniture, consider having a simple piece built. Antique furniture books provide pages of designs that can be easily copied.

For a light look in comfortable seating, use modular units covered with white slipcovers. These versatile seating units can be easily rearranged for a variety of different seating groups.

The idea is to keep your room simple and individual. Use your home as a showcase for crafts, natural objects, and things you and your children have made. Whatever collection you boast, a neutral background of light walls and softly colored furniture will show it to best advantage.

▲ *Handrubbed paneling in a family room complements the room's light color scheme. A light stain covers the oak floor. Pastels, light wood finishes, and fewer accessories update the country look.*

◄ *The yellow pine cabinet is a newly constructed antique reproduction. Its design and color add a light country accent to the room, without the expense of the antique piece.*

▲ *Quilts are integral accessories in a country scheme. Update your quilt display by placing your most treasured quilts in a Lucite trunk. Not only does it store and display your quilts, but it makes an excellent coffee table.*

▲ *Country crafts create a cozy ambience.*

▲ *In the same room, bold, contemporary colors and accessories are an ideal contrast to a neutral background.*

A Change of Style

When decorating your home, you make a definite statement about your tastes and lifestyle. Why not design your rooms so that when your decorating ideas or even the seasons change, your rooms can too — and with only a minimum amount of effort?

Take advantage of small details; in other words, let your accessories tell the story. Classically simple furniture styles, which adapt easily to a variety of room settings, work well as a background for an evolving display. Keeping the number of major pieces of furniture in a room to a minimum will lend importance to smaller articles.

When you use decorative objects as the focus, not the filler, choose pieces that are distinctive, yet compatible with one another. Mixing handcrafted items, whether new or antique, contemporary or primitive, is an excellent way to express individuality in decorating.

Create a gallerylike setting for your accessories by placing them against a neutral backdrop. Neutral-colored walls and furniture will complement your accessories, not compete with them. Gray, tan, peach, and ivory are versatile background colors that will enhance a variety of design schemes, regardless of the decorating style.

Change the accessories to evoke different moods in a room. Wooden decoys and Shaker bandboxes borrowed from the family room will lend a warm, comfortable feeling to a more formal living room. When used sparingly, bold decorative accents, such as an ebony bench or uplights placed under a large plant, will add refreshing contemporary style to a room. Even a simple change of accent pillows can make a dramatic color change.

▶ *Bring out the colors of contemporary crafts by placing less vibrant objects next to brighter ones.*

▲*Grouping similar items together is an excellent way to add strength to small pieces.*

91

▲ *For a fresh, springlike look, a white sofa is banked with pastel pillows. Oriental jars, silk flowers, and framed watercolors reinforce the pastel scheme.*

92

▲ *With a change of accessories, the same room echoes the rich colors of autumn. Baskets replace the shiny ceramic jars on the coffee table, and the pastel paintings are replaced with artwork in earthy hues.*

Creative Arrangements

Moving a piece of furniture to just the right spot can suddenly transform even a tiny room into a more comfortable, attractive, and useful space. Rearranging the furniture is also a quick and inexpensive way to redecorate. The same furnishings will look new when you arrange them in different, creative ways.

If you own an exceptionally beautiful or important piece of furniture, such as a hunt board or Welsh dresser, place it where it is visible from the entrance to a room. This placement creates an attractive point of interest opposite the door.

Arrange your furniture so that people circulate around and not through the seating areas. You can accomplish this "traffic control" by positioning furniture so that a pathway is created that starts at the room's entry, winds around the seating group, and ends at doors to other rooms.

With the proper arrangement, furniture can help to break up space and create angles in a small, boxy room. Instead of arranging furniture around the perimeter of the room, feature a special piece, such as a desk, by pulling it out perpendicular to the wall. Turn a sofa on a diagonal across a corner and fill the space behind it with a tall plant. Or for a contemporary room, you might add a triangular wooden cube table to fill the space behind the sofa.

A close arrangement of a few carefully selected furniture pieces can successfully open up a small space. For example, choose a love seat instead of a sofa, a glass-topped or mirrored table instead of a wooden coffee table. Rather than upholstered arm chairs, use a pair of wooden chairs. Keeping the number of accessories to a minimum will also contribute to the room's spacious feeling.

◄ *A pair of love seats, a wooden chair, and two stools are clustered around a coffee table, providing plenty of seating in a tight space. Built-in shelves offer abundant storage without using floor space. The mirrored wall creates an open, airy look and visually doubles the size of the room.*

◄*A wooden bench is positioned to create the sense of an entryway in an open room. Sparse accessories, a minimal use of fabric, and bare wood surfaces contribute to the uncluttered look of the small room.*

▲ *Two armless chairs, positioned together, form a perfect love seat. Long, decorative tassels tacked to the side of each chair help to reinforce the sense of one unit.*

▲*A bookcase-and-fireplace wall makes creative furniture arrangement a challenge. Placing the furniture at angles makes interesting use of the limited floor space.*

▲ *Contemporary seating creates a pleasing background for the display of Oriental art and accessories. Fabric on the wicker chairs repeats the blue background of the rice paper screen, helping to unify the arrangement.*

Drama on a Small Stage

There is no reason to let limited space restrict your potential for decorating in an original way. You can still set your sights high and create a very dramatic, individual look within a small area.

Especially when decorating tight spaces, it is important to decide upon a definite theme or direction and follow it closely when selecting the furnishings and accessories for your room. Whether you desire a rustic look with quilt-block pillows and weather-vane sculptures or an English country style with plump, chintz cushions and botanical prints, try not to compromise your selections. It is important to have a definite idea of the effect you want to achieve in your room.

In a small room, every detail is special. Since there is room for only a few pieces of furniture and relatively few accessories, each individual item plays a large part in completing the design scheme.

▲ English bamboo end tables and Oriental boxes and jars contribute color and detail to the room.

▲ A small Turkish rug adds pattern and deep color to the seating group. A pickled heart-pine trunk contributes storage space and makes an ideal coffee table. (Instructions for pickling furniture are in the Creative Design chapter.)

Create a Focal Point

Almost any room in your house can benefit from some type of focal point or strong center of visual interest. Some rooms already have architectural features, such as a fireplace or bay window, which you can use to anchor a furniture arrangement. In other rooms, special groupings composed of furniture, art, and accessories provide the interest.

Create a focal point where there is none by using the furniture and accessories you already have. In a small room, for example, you might call attention to a painted blanket chest by hanging a large framed poster above it. Use the surface of the chest for a changing display of pottery or other distinctive accessories.

With a pair of simple bookshelf units, you can add architectural interest and make a feature of an entire wall. Place a bookshelf at each end of the wall, paint the shelves and wall the same color, and fill the space between the shelf units with a low chest of drawers or a table. The result is an easily created focal point that has the intriguing look of a built-in unit.

There is no more appropriate focal point for a room than a handmade object of your own design. Whatever your favorite crafts may be, your handwork will make an excellent addition to a room. Consider painting one wall in your room a bright color to complement a special quilt used as a wall hanging. A grouping of framed, cross-stitched samplers hung above a table is a good way both to decorate your room and to display your own work.

◀ *Bookshelf units painted the same color as the wall and placed on either side of a low chest transform the entire wall into an interesting focal point for the room.*

► *An artful array presents a refined, attractive point of interest in a foyer. The tray and boxes help to balance the long, tapering legs of the Sheraton mahogany table, while also hiding the plugs and cords along the baseboard. An Art Nouveau vase filled with dried grass helps connect the carved Indian panel with the table and accessories.*

▼ *A handsome piece of furniture, a deep wall color, and dramatic lighting create a strong focal point when used opposite the entrance to a room.*

► *The coral striations of the wallpaper provide the background for a collection of old prints, making a striking focal point of a wall in a narrow study.*

▲ *A special piece of furniture, such as a painted blanket chest, holds a changing display of baskets and other accessories. A framed poster enhances the arrangement.*

104

▲ *The fireplace wall is designed to be an area of major visual interest, and it is a good spot to display a distinctive, one-of-a-kind accessory. If your room has a decorative, nonworking fireplace, use the opening as a backdrop for a dramatic still-life arrangement.*

Focus on the Fireplace

Most fireplaces look more complete with a painting hung on the chimneypiece and a few accessories arranged on the mantel. However, your mantel arrangement need not remain the same forever. To be a continual source of pleasure, your treasures should be occasionally rearranged. Use your imagination to make the fireplace an ever-changing display to suit your moods, the seasons, or the special occasion.

▼ *Use a fanciful display of miniatures to add a touch of fun and whimsy to the mantelpiece.*

▲*A grouping of stylishly overscale painted cutouts is a lighthearted approach to covering the fireplace opening in warm months. (Instructions for making the cutouts are in the Creative Design chapter.)*

▲ *Mirrors cover old, cracked tiles around a fireplace open-ing for a sleek, new look.*

▲ *In summer, replace the glow of a fire with a richly colored fire screen. (Instructions for papering a fire screen are in the Creative Design chapter.)*

▲ *A narrow mirror hung horizontally works beautifully over an unusually tall mantelpiece. The tall vases add symmetry to the mantel arrangement and echo the vivid blue color of the fire screen.*

▲ *For a classic look, keep mantel accessories in symmetrical balance by using a pair of objects, such as candlesticks or vases, one at each end of the mantelpiece. Vary the classic look by featuring an assortment of collectibles in the center of the mantel, instead of just one accessory.*

107

Storage from the Past

Large pieces of furniture, such as wardrobes and armoires, are versatile, practical, and can be adapted for storage in almost any room of the house. In a room with no major architectural feature, the armoire can become an attractive focal point. When placed opposite a wide doorway or a bay window, it helps to balance the room, and because of its height, the armoire adds a stately presence to any decor.

If you have an armoire that is in less-than-mint condition, there are a variety of ways to improve its appearance. Damaged doors can be replaced with pieces of plain or beveled glass. Or for a new look, try replacing the old doors with lattice panels. If the surface of the armoire is scratched or marred, try bleaching, stripping, refinishing, or painting it for a fresh finish.

Tips for using armoires in new ways:
*For use as a television or stereo cabinet, drill a hole in the back of the cabinet in an inconspicuous corner to run the electrical cords out the back to the wall socket.
*To display your favorite collections, line the inside of the armoire with fabric, place your collectibles on the shelves, and leave the doors open.
*For a sparkling, glittering bar, mirror the back panel of the cabinet. Hang one shelf at counter height (approximately thirty-six inches from the floor) and use narrow shelves above to leave room to work. Place bottles on lower shelves, glassware on upper shelves.
*To use in the kitchen, paint the armoire in a bright color and use it to hold cookbooks, casseroles, and china.
*For an attractive storage space, use the top of the armoire for display. Let baskets or an arrangement of dried plants bridge the gap between the top of the armoire and the ceiling.

▲ *Lattice doors and a new, lighter wood finish add a contemporary look to an old armoire.*

▶ *A fabric-backed Shaker cabinet in the dining room makes it possible to keep china and serving pieces conveniently near the table. A small lamp adds a warm glow to the shelves.*

▲ *Armoires serve well as bookcases or as storage and display units. They can also provide a good hiding place for the television.*

▶ *Widely spaced shelves in a pine armoire accommodate stacks of antique quilts, while woven baskets neatly organize sewing supplies.*

Choose the
Right Area Rug

Whether it is a cozy rag, a sturdy wool, or an elegant kilim, an area rug is one of the most useful accessories in a room. Aside from merely covering the floor, a rug adds mood, texture, and color to any space. Area rugs can unite rooms, define specific spaces, bind diverse furnishings, tie color schemes together, and act as focal points. They can even be used on top of wall-to-wall carpet to spark

a bit of color interest, add pattern, or even cover a worn spot.

Regardless of function, the first step in choosing an area rug is to fit it to the room and the furniture. If possible, furniture should either be placed entirely on an area rug or entirely off it. For example, consider a rectangular living room. The furniture on two sides is against the walls; on the other two sides, the furniture sits three feet away from the walls. A rug that fits under the legs of all the furniture would be pleasing. But if all furniture is placed against the wall, the same rug would be distractingly small.

▲ An antique Persian rug suits a sophisticated dining room. The subtle patterns lend color and design, and the carpet is a perfect size—chair legs stay on the rug when chairs are pulled from the table.

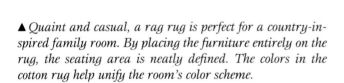

▲ Quaint and casual, a rag rug is perfect for a country-in-spired family room. By placing the furniture entirely on the rug, the seating area is neatly defined. The colors in the cotton rug help unify the room's color scheme.

To determine the size of a rug for a dining area, add thirty inches beyond the table edge on all sides. This allowance ensures that chair legs will be on the rug when the chairs are pushed back.

In the bedroom, you may choose to put the rug either under or next to the bed. Ideally, a rug should extend at least to the foot of the bed and about thirty-five inches out from the side.

▲ A rosy wool rug enhances the mood of the room. An area rug in a bedroom should extend to the foot of the bed and about a yard from the side.

▲ *An uplight placed on the floor behind a display pedestal adds drama to a collection of ceramics.*

▶ *Shaded candles can provide subtle accent lighting where you would not ordinarily put an electric lamp. Placed on a coffee table, a shaded candle emits a soft glow in the center of a seating area, while lamps on the end tables illuminate the outer perimeter of the grouping.*

Accent with Soft Lighting

Several areas of indirect light in a room create soft contrasts that are far more pleasing than light from a single overhead fixture. The proper light can brighten a corner, emphasize a painting or plant, or enable you to read with ease. Having several light sources in a room also allows you the flexibility of changing the level of light for different activities, such as entertaining or sewing.

Every room needs some type of general lighting—the background light that is reflected from the walls and ceiling. Central overhead fixtures offer good, even light, but not much character. Several table lamps spaced around a room will provide adequate general lighting in a much more decorative fashion.

Accent lighting adds personality and drama to a room. Tucked away in unusual places, accent lights can illuminate special areas that would otherwise go unnoticed. A canister light positioned at the base of a plant will create dramatic shadows of the foliage. Small portrait lights can be used to brighten paintings, while at the same time increasing the overall level of light in the room. You can also add points of light around a room by using small lamps to brighten the interior of shelves and cabinets. Accent lights placed atop a cabinet or bookshelf will provide a dramatic backlight for plants or baskets.

Task lighting is useful in areas where you sew, read, or do other close work. This type of lighting works best when balanced with adequate background lighting. The task light can be directed at your book or sewing, while the general light reduces the glare.

▲ *A candlestick lamp attractively accents both the painting and the tabletop arrangement. The tall, slender shape of the lamp is the proper scale for the small table surface.*

◄ *A Staffordshire lamp casts a soft glow in a china hutch, while providing good light for reading. A small portrait light spotlights a painting and creates a pleasing point of interest at the top of the hutch.*

More than a Sunroom

A sunroom can be the most welcoming room in the house. Regardless of the decor, the warm glow of sunlight creates a calm and comfortable environment, perfect for sitting back and relaxing. With the right combination of furnishings and accessories, your sunroom can be anything—with a table and chairs, it is the ideal spot for a small luncheon; with a daybed, it becomes a guest room; add a few shelves, and suddenly you have a sun-drenched library.

Natural elements, such as wicker furniture and lush greenery, enhance the open look and feel of the room. If your sunroom is an extension of a larger, more formal room, the transition from one room to the other may be a problem. To smooth the transition, consider using the same flooring throughout the two rooms. Or for a unified appearance, use an area rug in your sunroom that repeats strong accent colors from your living area.

Not everything in the sunroom has to be casual. Feature an elegant coffee table or a grouping of prints in your room for a dressed-up look. Arranging wicker furniture and upholstered pieces together makes a striking grouping, while adding a formal touch to your sunroom. Use the same fabric on your upholstered furniture and wicker chair cushions to unify the two styles.

The sunroom is also a perfect place to express your creative flair. Let your wicker furniture make a strong statement by painting it a bright, bold hue. Painting a woven sisal rug is another clever, inexpensive way to add exactly the colors needed to complement your room's decor.

▲ *A rock wall, a lattice "chair rail," and soft, fabric cushions add a touch of indoor comfort to a screened sunroom, while retaining the cool, airiness of outdoors. Painting an inexpensive woven sisal rug with fabric dye can transform it into a custom-matched accent rug. (Instructions for painting a rug with fabric dye are in the Creative Design chapter.)*

▲ *Victorian wicker mixes easily with Queen Anne and French furniture for a feeling of casual elegance. Using the same fabric on the love seat and wicker chair cushions unifies the look of the different styles of furniture. Elements from the adjoining living room—such as the paintings on the brick wall, the delicate porcelain vase and bowl, and the area rug on the tile floor—help give the feeling of one large living area instead of a sunroom addition.*

◄*A grouping of Audubon prints and antique white wicker reinforces the open, airy mood of a sunroom-turned-library.*

Bedrooms

Your bedroom can be a private retreat, complete with a sofa and easy chair; or furnished with a daybed, it may double as a den or office. With a few simple decorating ideas, you can arrange and decorate your room, regardless of its size, with a fresh spark of creativity.

▲ *A quilt at the foot of the bed sets the color theme for a bedroom, while accessories add polish.*

Master Bedroom Retreats

A master bedroom can offer more than room for sleeping. By adding a couple of comfortable chairs, a table, and a lamp in a cozy corner, you can transform your bedroom into a private retreat.

To update a tired-looking bedroom, try removing typical bedroom pieces from the room. To provide additional floor space in your bedroom, put the chest of drawers in the closet or replace it with inexpensive, stacked storage units that fit in the closet; then pull furniture from other parts of the house into the bedroom to create a small sitting area. Cover bedside tables with round tops and full, fabric skirts to give a new look to dated nightstands.

Even if the bedroom is small, you can add seating with a love seat or an easy chair. Include a lamp and a well-stocked bookcase, and you have a quiet, comfortable spot for reading and relaxing. Simple pieces of furniture, such as a desk or worktable, can turn an area of your bedroom into a private work space. Add an armoire for an elegant way to house a television or stereo unit.

An asymmetrical furniture arrangement will relax the stiff appearance of matched sets of furniture. An antique piece also contributes a visual contrast that will blend easily with different styles of furniture. Wicker or rattan furnishings are a good choice for small bedrooms, because of their airy appearance. And because they are lightweight, wicker chairs can be easily repositioned for watching television or sitting closer to a window for natural light.

▲ *A bedroom fireplace is the focus of the sitting area.*

▲ *The adjoining bath continues the color scheme and mood of the bedroom.*

▲ *Natural wood furnishings, white walls, and light-colored draperies contribute to the bedroom's spacious look, while the comforter, pillows, and rug add color and pattern.*

▶ *Two twig chairs, a small table, and a large potted plant are all that is needed to transform a tiny alcove into a cozy conversation area.*

◄ *Slipcovered easy chairs are an inexpensive way to fashion a bedroom sitting area and to introduce colorful pattern into the room. Positioning the chairs so that they face each other requires a minimum amount of floor space and makes an intimate spot for conversation.*

▼ *The slipcover fabric also covers the bedside tables.*

▲ *A sewing machine in the corner of a bedroom is the center of a craftsman's retreat.*

▲ *An adjoining bathroom furnished with a footed tub, braided rug, and polished antique furniture can be a luxurious extension of the master suite.*

◄ *The quilts and rag rugs surrounding the bed reflect the creative appeal of the sewing area.*

125

Create a Country French Look

The essence of country French is a look that is a bit frivolous but not fussy, with soft colors, furniture with gracefully curving lines, and carefully selected accessories. Bedrooms are especially suited to this look, which is distinguished by yards of ribbon and lace, iron and brass furniture, baskets, decorative straw hats, and tiny print fabrics and wallpapers.

To bring a touch of the country French look to your own home, add lace or eyelet to pillows, window treatments, and table skirts. Fill natural baskets with dried, silk, or fresh wildflowers. Or choose wallpapers in small floral or foulard prints. Just a hint of country French blends best with traditional or colonial-style rooms.

As with any decorating scheme, attention to detail is important in evoking a country French mood. Mauve, rose, celadon green, and larkspur blue are characteristic colors of this style. Use these colors in wallpaper, upholstery fabrics, and draperies.

An old-fashioned lamp or antique dresser set will seem right at home in a country French room, as will photographs displayed in pretty ribbon-trimmed frames. Use delicate porcelain containers to hold jewelry and other small items on a desk or dresser. Paper-covered hatboxes, delicate botanical prints, and a scattering of flowers and baskets will add a distinctive touch.

▲ *Hatboxes covered in wallpaper and trimmed with ribbon are decorative elements that also provide attractive storage space. A botanical print was dressed up in a manner befitting the country French style by placing a velvet bow above the picture.*

▼ *Brass furniture, lace and ribbon accents, and floral wallpaper all suggest a country French theme.*

▲ *A delicate table skirt was fashioned by simply sewing four lace napkins together, with two-inch-wide grosgrain ribbons added to cover the seams. Decorative bows were tacked in place.*

Daybeds for Sitting & Sleeping

A daybed can be the perfect solution to a common decorating dilemma. A versatile daybed gives you additional sleeping space without requiring an extra bedroom. Any spare room can double as a year-round studio, sewing area, or work room and still provide a comfortable bedroom for guests.

Most daybeds are twin size (thirty-nine inches wide, seventy-five inches long) and can use standard twin-size mattresses and bedding. Antique daybeds may require custom-made mattresses, since they often vary from today's standard sizes. You should consider the added cost of a special mattress before purchasing a "bargain" antique.

Cot-width or dormitory-width mattresses (thirty, thirty-three, and thirty-six inches) may fit an antique bed, but the cheapest and easiest way to get a mattress for an odd-sized antique is to cut a thick foam rubber sheet to the bed's exact size. Standard fitted sheets can be altered with elastic or tucking for a tighter fit. Since daybeds are deeper than standard couches, add plenty of well-stuffed pillows for comfortable back support.

You can easily decorate a daybed to blend with the look of a room. Create a delicate, romantic look with lacy pillow shams, a full dust ruffle, and a pastel quilt. Neat plaid covers with matching curtains and upholstery fabric create a tailored appearance, perfect for a boy's bedroom or a den.

▼ *An antique metal daybed is not practical for seating because of its decorative front railing, but its handsome Victorian style is well suited to an attic guest room.*

▲ *A ruffled coverlet conceals a pull-out trundle bed. The lacy shams and coverlet create a soft, romantic look.*

▲ *On a Chinese Chippendale-style daybed, the lightly pickled finish creates a relaxed formality in a small living room. Chintz and canvas cushions fill out the back of the daybed, making it comfortable for sitting.*

Fashion a Stylish Bedspread

▲ *The pastel beauty of a painted throw and coordinating sheets was inspired by the delicate floral designs woven into the damask. (Instructions for painting a damask throw are in the Creative Design chapter.)*

Sets of coordinated bed linens can give your bedroom a look of high style, but at a high price. Bedspreads and quilts, the most visible and important bedroom fashions, are usually the most expensive items in making a bed. You can avoid some of the cost and still enjoy a fashionable look in your bedroom by creating your own bedspread.

One easy way to make a lightweight bedspread is to stitch two matching flat sheets together, using one for the top and one for the lining. A bedspread made this way can be placed over a sheet in warm weather, over a blanket when the weather is cool. The bedspread works best when it is made of

◀ *A bedspread made from sheets is an ideal way to give your bedroom an entirely new look at a low cost. (Instructions for sewing a bedspread from sheets are in the Creative Design chapter.)*

dark-colored sheets. To determine if a patterned sheet with a light background is opaque enough to use, place two thicknesses of the sheet wrong sides together to see if the pattern of the sheet underneath shows through on top. If it is visible, then use a matching solid sheet as a lining. Purchase additional sheets in the same design as the spread to use on the bed for a luscious, coordinated look.

Even an old damask tablecloth can make an exquisite summer throw. It is easy to create a singularly beautiful effect by painting in the floral or geometric designs already woven into the damask. And when used as a bed throw, painted damask can be particularly striking, because it becomes the basis for an entire decorating scheme.

Instructions for sewing a bedspread from flat sheets and for painting a damask throw are in the Creative Design chapter.

▲ *A small heart-shaped pillow was made from the corner section of an old tablecloth. Drawn threadwork forms chevrons that accent the pillow's shape, and the crocheted border, from another piece of old linen, adds a frilly edge.*

▼ *Antique lace adds a luxurious look to a makeshift dressing table. (Instructions for making a round tablecloth are in the Creative Design chapter.)*

Focus on Lace & Linens

Vintage linens and lace are far too pretty to hide in a drawer. Their gossamer beauty adds a dreamy touch of nostalgia to any decor and is especially suited to bedrooms. With a little creative sewing, you can mend damaged fabrics with touches of embroidery and bits of linen and lace, turning wonderful old pieces into lovely decorative accents for your room.

▲ The seams of old pillowcases were opened, a small casing was sewn, and the pillowcases were gathered on a rod to make lovely, lacy cafe curtains.

▲ An ecru crocheted table runner is secured with pushpins along the frame of an odd-shaped window.

▲ A Continental sham was made from a cutwork bridge cloth. The cloth was lined with fabric to cover the open areas and then backed with more fabric to make the case. Lace napkins make lovely small pillows to scatter around the sham.

Finishing Touches

Once the major elements of a room are in place, add the important details, such as a special window treatment or a fancy painted wall finish. Innovative arrangements of your favorite china, prints, and collectibles will also lend a special touch to your room settings.

Innovative Windows

Window treatments can provide the major impact in a decorating scheme and often are just the finishing touch your room needs. Lacy curtains tied with satiny ribbons set a frilly mood in a little girl's room, while a fabric-covered cornice adds a quiet touch of sophistication to a hallway window. Easy no-sew window treatments update ordinary windows with contemporary flair. And a dainty bridge cloth covers a window with surprising, innovative style.

▲ *A lovely, delicate curtain can be fashioned from a lacy bridge cloth. Fold the cloth diagonally over a spring-tension rod, tacking at the edges to hold the cloth in place. Then, simply fold up the front corner, add a decorative tassel, and tack the layers of cloth together.*

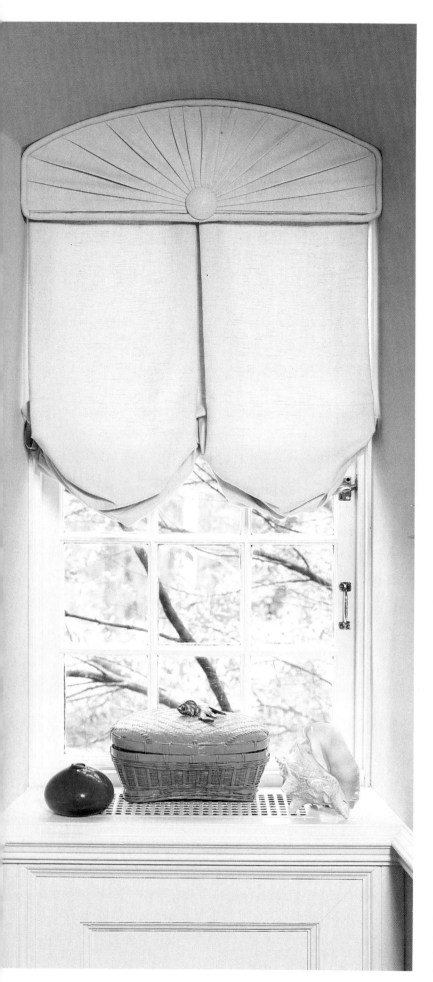

◄ *A cornice board cut from plywood and covered with fabric creates a sophisticated window treatment. Fan-shaped pleats are stapled in place. A large fabric-covered button hides the staples, and thick cording around the edge helps fill any gaps between the cornice and the wall.*

▲ *A stylish look is achieved by finger-pleating curtains and then tying them at the top with rubber bands, which are looped over a nail at the corner of the window. A large knot, tied from fabric made plump with polyester stuffing, is positioned on a nail to hide the curtain heading. Wide molding substitutes for a valance. (Instructions for tying the fabric knot are in the Creative Design chapter.)*

► *Two lengths of contrasting fabric twisted together soften a large window. The amount of fabric needed for this treatment is three times the width of the window, plus two times the height from the floor to the rod.*

▼ *Striped denim accentuates the contours of an innovative valance. Oversize bows are glued to clothespins and then used to clip the swag to the rod. Curtains are made from sheeting and utilize existing hems. (Instructions for draping the swag are in the Creative Design chapter.)*

▲ *Embroidered fabric is shirred to a band of cotton lace, then tied with narrow ribbons to fabric-covered rods to make a dainty curtain.*

◄ *A valance is mounted on a thin, flexible board and attached inside the window frame. Gathers are made by sewing Roman shade tape to the back of the valance and shirring it with cords.*

▲ *A width of fabric is looped over a PVC pipe to give a poufed swag visual weight. Bows anchor the swag, while adding a decorative touch. (Instructions for making the swag are in the Creative Design chapter.)*

Fancy Walls

You can capture the exotic mood of stone archways, romantic vistas, and indoor orangeries in your own home. Such grand features are as near as a blank wall, a talented artist, and a creative trompe l'oeil plan. Or, if you prefer a more subtle wall treatment, create your own design with easy hand-painted finishes. You can even skip the hand painting and get the same look with wallpapers that emulate the look once achieved only by hand.

▶ *Painted stones frame an otherwise undistinguished bedroom window, giving it character and depth.*

▼ *The bedroom walls are stippled, an effect that makes the stones painted around the window even more realistic.*

140

◄ *Books and mementos are realistically painted on the front of a medicine cabinet, adding an unconventional touch to a conventional bathroom.*

▲ *A delicate orange tree freshens a corner.*

◄ *Colorful flowers "bloom" in an array of vases painted along a bathroom wall.*

141

▲ *A formal foyer boasts a hand-painted wall with an unusual and flattering pink and white color scheme. (Instructions for hand painting walls are in the Creative Design chapter.)*

▼ *Bright pink was combed in a random pattern over white. A second coat of white combed in wavy lines was topped by a coat of polyurethane varnish.*

▲ *Sponge painting below a painted chair rail adds richness and texture to a spacious entryway. (Instructions for sponge painting walls are in the Creative Design chapter.)*

142

▲ Wallpaper can simulate the textured look once achieved only by hand painting.

◄ Spatterware-look wallpaper duplicates an old hand-painting technique which involves free-form speckling of different shades of paint.

Creative Displays

One of life's pleasures is collecting the things you love. But too often, precious possessions are difficult to display and end up stuffed into closets and cabinets, away from where you can delight in their beauty and the memories they evoke. Bring out your treasured collectibles and arrange them in exciting, new ways.

▲ *A wide silk ribbon, topped by a sumptuous rosette, adds dramatic impact to two prints.*

◄ *A large, symmetrical arrangement of botanical prints is the ideal counterpart to large-scale furniture.*

◀ *Gleaming copper adds warm highlights to a collection of birds' nests, paintings, and dried flowers.*

▲ *A mantelpiece showcases a tasteful arrangement of porcelain plates and unmatched china teacups.*

◀ *Matching plates provide a cohesive visual link from a low chest to an eye-level mirror above.*

▲ Six framed prints, ingeniously hung above a doorway, tie the colors and mood of the dining room in with a nearby entry hall.

▲ Shirred fabric provides an ideal backdrop for displaying delicate china plates.

▶ Staffordshire and Chinese export platters transform a wall into a showcase. The china's blue-and-white motif is echoed by the platter and the smaller accent pieces on the English mule chest.

148

◄ A powder room becomes a minigallery as a light hidden under the counter spotlights a collection of small art objects and Indian dolls.

▼ Layering a collection of paisley shawls on an old ladder accentuates their intricate patterns and textures.

Tabletop Displays

A bare tabletop is like a blank canvas. Take advantage of this space to arrange your finest accessories and prettiest collectibles into dramatic, mood-setting displays. When creating tabletop arrangements of your cherished objects, consider the color, pattern, and shape of each piece to achieve a balanced overall effect. Too many dark colors or large pieces grouped together will have a heavy appearance; too many light colors or small objects will look insubstantial.

▶ *A deep blue wall enhances an exquisite tabletop display of blue-and-white glazed china. The framed print repeats the collection's Oriental motif.*

▲ *Bases of varying heights are used to draw attention to individual pieces in a still-life arrangement. Using both large and small objects adds visual variety to the tabletop display.*

▲ *A botanical print, accented with a ribbon rosette, balances a delicate display of small objects. The print is hung low over the table, giving the impression that it is a part of the tabletop arrangement.*

▶ *A small lace-and-linen square gives emphasis to a simple bedside table arrangement.*

◄ Seashells form an intriguing, seasonal still life. A clear glass hurricane shade and a painted plate stand organize the display.

▲ A tabletop stack of oversize books doubles as an attractive end table.

◄ Dark wooden bases, low-key in size, material, and finish, do not distract from the objects displayed.

153

Delicate Details

The most important ingredient in your home's decor is something that makes it individual — the delicate detail that shows your very personal way of doing things. It does not have to be a bold or elaborate statement, but just a touch that will give your home a sense of special style.

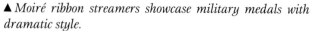

▲ *Moiré ribbon streamers showcase military medals with dramatic style.*

▼ *Epaulets gracefully flank a regal portrait, and a decorative sword takes a position of prominence in a room accented with military mementos.*

▲ An opulent bedroom is enhanced by rich colors and textures. A hand-pleated fan, made from the window shade fabric, graces the top of a framed coat-of-arms.

◀ A panel of fabric stapled to the wall creates an innovative border. Strip molding, nailed in place, covers the staples.

▶ *Two paintings hang gracefully from a ribbon attached to the window facing in an enchanting summer room. The paintings are backed with dark green fabric to create an attractive view from outside, as well.*

▼ *A deliciously detailed table skirt and pillows add a fresh touch of color. (Instructions for making the table skirt with shirred welt and the knot for the pillows are in the Creative Design chapter.)*

▲ *A small piece of artwork, hung on the wall of a bookcase, attractively fills a gap between shelves.*

▲ *Glass vials with suction cups attached display dried or fresh flowers with creative flair.*

▲ *Small crystal accessories add to the polished, sophisticated look of a marble-topped wash basin.*

▲ *A cordial glass becomes a dainty miniature vase when filled with a handful of small flowers.*

▲ *Lacy table runners, colorful dinner napkins, even stylish silk scarves can be pressed into service to give your pillows new life, while adding a fresh look to your room. Simple knots, ribbons, and pins keep the covers in place. (Instructions for tied pillow covers are in the Creative Design chapter.)*

Creative Design

There is a bit of the artist in each of us. Who has not looked admiringly at a fabulous paint color or a length of pretty fabric and wished for an easy and really creative way to use it? Give your home a splash of creativity with our easy-to-follow instructions.

Hand-Painted Walls

▲ *No special training is needed to create an intricately textured, combed wall finish.*

Combing, sponging, and striating are wall painting techniques that are easy to execute with no special training. After a base coat of paint, the second coat is applied with an implement (a comb, sponge, or paintbrush) that gives the desired pattern and texture.

The choice of paints includes flat and satin-finish (semi-gloss) oil or oil-base paint; flat and semi-gloss latex paint; and glaze. Glazing liquid has a syrupy consistency and can be colored with universal tints (concentrated pigment that is mixed with paint to give color). Glazing liquid dries transparent with a satin finish, and the color beneath will show through. Since glaze is slow to dry, you can take your time working with it. Interesting effects can be achieved by overlapping colored glazes, such as pale blue and pink. The overlapped areas then become lavender or violet.

Universal tints come in a wide range of colors and can be added to glaze, oil, latex, and acrylic paints. However, a little tint goes a long way. Tint is best used for tinting glaze and white paint. For deeper tones, it is easier to select colors from the paint charts and have the paint mixed at the store.

Before you tackle a wall, try out color and technique by painting on a large scrap of Sheetrock. (Ask at a lumber yard for a damaged piece.)

Prepare the walls as you would for a regular paint job. Wash the surface to remove soil or grease, fill in holes with spackle, and sand the wall smooth. Paint with a primer-sealer if the wall is new or has been previously painted a dark color.

Combing

You can make a comb from a piece of vinyl floor tile, sheet metal, or a window cleaners' squeegee. (A 6-inch squeegee is easy to use because it has a handle and is short enough to be easily cut.) Cut notches in the edge with a utility knife or tin snips. Notches can be thin points up to about ⅜-inch wide, evenly or irregularly spaced.

Apply the base coat to the walls to be painted. After the base coat has dried, apply a second coat. Roll or brush the second coat of paint on the wall in 2- to 3-foot-wide sections and comb it while still wet. Drag the comb through the wet paint or glaze, leaving a straight trail (as striped) or one that is wiggly and random. If you make a mistake, brush out the area and repeat the combing step. Wipe the comb off frequently to prevent paint build-up.

Combing can be done with one combed coat of paint or glaze over a base coat. Or you can add successive combed coats in varying shades of color, letting each coat dry completely before adding the next. For a single combed coat, tinted glaze offers a soft, subtle effect.

Sponging

Sponging involves thinning the second coat of paint or glaze and dabbing it lightly on the wall with a sponge. Use a natural sponge torn into a convenient size and shape. With gloved hands, dip the sponge in paint, then wring it out so that excess paint will not blob or run down the wall. Pounce (a light up-and-down motion) the sponge lightly and evenly on the wall, working in 3-foot-square areas and stepping back often to be sure the effect is even. You can go over the same area a second time to even out the texture. If you are working with more than one color, allow the previous coat to dry before proceeding. A build-up of several related colors, such as blue-lavender-pink, yellow-orange-red, or beige-grey-white, can be

very subtle and interesting. After rinsing one color from the sponge, be sure the sponge is thoroughly wrung out, so that the next paint color is not thinned too much. Before applying successive colors on the wall, test each series of pounces on newspaper to be sure it will match the previous series.

Striating & Drybrushing

For a striated finish, apply a thin coat of paint or glaze over the base coat, then wipe the brush on a cloth and pull it through the paint, leaving long even brush strokes for texture.

Drybrushing is a slightly different technique. Barely dip the brush in the paint and apply it in light feathery strokes over the base coat. For "antiquing" or striating paneled wallboard, oil-base semi-gloss drybrushed right over the wallboard finish works best.

The texture of the striating depends on the coarseness of the brush. If the paintbrush does not provide enough texture, drag a hairbrush or scrub brush through the wet paint on the wall. Use paint sparingly to keep from producing solid areas. If you make a mistake, a section may be wiped off with a rag moistened with water or paint thinner (depending on the type of paint you are using), but the background may have been tinted by the first coat and may show through the final coat.

The Paints to Use

Technique	Paint	Characteristics
Combing	Base coat: Latex semi-gloss	Easiest to use Dries quickly
	Second coat: Latex semi-gloss	Lots of texture Cleans up with water
	Base: Oil semi-gloss Second: Glaze (thin coat)	Soft subtle effect
	Base: Oil semi-gloss Second: Oil or oil-base	Texture flatter More difficult to clean up
Sponging	Base: Flat oil-base Second: Oil flat or semi-gloss	A flat second coat will blend into flat base coat
	Base: Flat latex Second: Semi-gloss latex	A semi-gloss second will give more contrast to base coat
Striating	Base: Oil-base semi-gloss Second: Glaze or oil-base	Subtle color. Streaks of brush strokes allow base coat to show through
Drybrushing	Base: Latex semi-gloss Second: Latex or acrylic	Feathery brush strokes over base coat

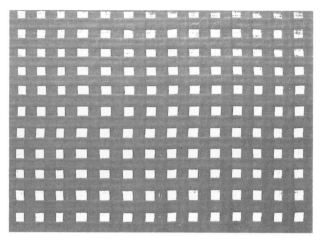

▲ Rust-colored latex semi-gloss was combed first in stripes over a beige base coat. A second coat was combed in the opposite direction, forming a basket-weave pattern.

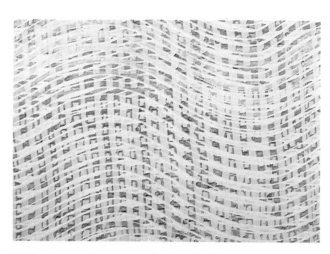

▲ Blue latex paint was combed in a basket-weave pattern on a white base coat. The same pattern was combed again with white paint, but with wavy horizontal lines.

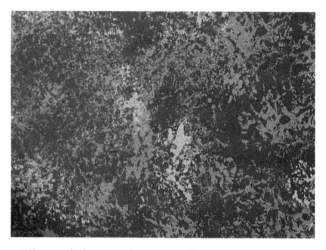

▲ Lilac and then peach were applied in successive layers with a natural sponge over a base coat of plum, giving the impression of a hand-painted paper.

▲ Acrylic paint in green and blue was drybrushed over semi-gloss oil-base paint. Feathery strokes in all directions create a striking effect.

▲ Thinned lavender oil paint was drybrushed on a semi-gloss oil-base coat. While the paint was still wet, more texture was added by dragging broomstraws in a wiggly pattern in the same direction as the brush strokes.

◄ For your kitchen, choose a stencil design that fits the area. Select colors to blend with the existing decor.

Stenciled Backsplash

A stenciled backsplash cover is an easy and inexpensive way to add new color and design to your kitchen. Cut from hardboard and protected with coats of clear sealer, it can endure work-a-day accidents and come clean with the wipe of a cloth. Best of all, you do not have to work in an awkward position while making this project. It can be done on a flat surface and then attached to the wall.

To make the backsplash, cut ⅛-inch hardboard to fit the backsplash area. If there are electrical outlets, measure carefully and cut out openings. If the area to be covered is large, cut the board in even sections between designs for ease in handling. Sand the edges. Apply three coats of flat latex paint to the front and sides. (Note: Gloss or satin paint is more difficult to stencil.)

Adjust your stencil, enlarging or reducing it to fit your space. (Instructions for making your own stencils are in the section on stenciling walls.) Cut a separate stencil for each color you are planning to use. Cut out registration circles in the corners as guides for positioning each stencil in turn. Place the first stencil on the board and tape it in place. Place a very small piece of masking tape inside each registration circle and leave it in place until all the colors are stenciled.

Apply the first color of paint to the open areas of the stencil with an up-and-down motion of the stencil brush. Try not to get paint under the stencil. When the entire color area has been covered, remove the stencil and wipe the back clean. Tape the stencil to the next section to be painted and continue with the first color for all subsequent

"tiles." (Note: Be sure to make registration circles for each repeat.) For each color, start with the first tile and proceed in the manner outlined above.

When stenciling is complete, remove the masking tape used for registration. With a waterproof marker and a ruler, make faint lines between stenciled sections to give the appearance of separate tiles. Apply several coats of clear acrylic spray. Attach the backsplash to the wall with small nails.

163

Stenciled Walls

Stencils can be purchased, or you can make your own. To make a stencil, select your design from fabric, wallpaper, a book, or any traceable source. For ease in stenciling, the part of the design you copy should be of a manageable size, approximately 6 to 8 inches square.

Place a piece of tracing paper over the design. Trace the main shapes, keeping them simple. The shapes should be individual and should not overlap or touch. (For a good illustration of how a flower motif from fabric might be adapted to a stencil design, see page 185.)

Next, place a piece of acetate (available at art supply stores) over the traced design. Cut a separate stencil for each color you are planning to use. For example, a design with two colors will require two stencils, and so on. (As an alternative, use one stencil and cover the open areas not being painted with masking tape.) Using a sharp craft knife, cut away only those areas of the design that will be of one color. Work on a cutting board, keep a firm pressure on the knife, try to make one continuous cut, and be sure cuts at the corners are clean.

To hold the stencil together, leave narrow strips of acetate between the openings in the stencil design. If you cut through the acetate strip, repair the stencil on both sides with cellophane tape. Use a craft knife to trim the excess tape.

Use the stencils in sequence. When the first color has dried, overlay the next stencil and apply the second color. (When using one stencil for all of the colors, mask off with tape the colors not being painted at that time, then paint the open areas of the design.)

Smooth walls freshly painted with flat or semi-gloss paint make an ideal surface for stenciling. Measure the walls and mark the placement of the design. If you are planning to extend a band of stenciling around the room, try to make the beginning and end of the design merge unnoticeably. Use a plumb line to mark the wall so that your

▲ *A stenciled garland adds subtle detail to a family room.*

lines will be straight. And be sure to have some of the background color on hand for touch-ups.

Practice stenciling the design first on paper. Then position the stencil on the wall and use a bit of masking tape to help hold the stencil pattern in place. Apply light layers of artists' acrylic paint (either in jars or tubes) with a short, stiff-bristled stencil brush. Use a little paint at a time, dabbing it on with an up-and-down motion, and keep the brush dry for a soft, pretty look. Add paint gradually, until you reach the color you desire. Clean the front and back edges of the stencils after each color has been stenciled, to prevent build-up and smearing of the paint.

▶ *Repeating an element of the stencil design on the draperies enhances the decorative effect of the stenciling.*

165

Windows

Window Shades

Canvas Shade

A fabric shade that fits within a window frame is easy to make from canvas or any heavy fabric. To begin, measure the length and width of the window, taking your measurements inside the window frame. Add 3 inches to the width and 8 inches to the length. Cut the fabric for the shade and the lining to these dimensions.

Place the shade fabric and the lining right sides together. Stitch the two fabrics together, 1½ inches from the side edges and 3 inches from the bottom edge. Turn the shade right side out and press.

Cut two strips of Roman shade ring tape to the length of the shade plus 6 inches. Pin the strips of ring tape to the back of the shade so that the first ring on each strip of tape is approximately 1 inch from the bottom edge of the shade. Below the bottom ring, turn a bit of extra tape against the lining. Machine-stitch through both layers of fabric along each edge of the tape. Trim any extra tape from the top of the shade.

Cut a length of 1- x 2-inch wood to fit inside the window frame. Paint the wood white or a color to match your fabric.

Wrap the top of the shade once around the strip of wood, as shown in the diagram, and tack the fabric in place. At each end of the wood strip, insert a screw eye close to the ring tape.

To hang the shade, position the wood strip at the top of the window and run a long wood screw through the wood into the top window casing.

Tie a piece of lightweight traverse cord or Roman shade cord to the bottom ring on each side of the shade. Run cording up through the loops, through the screw eyes, and to one side of the window. Pull the cording to give equal tension, adjust to reduce slack, and cut the excess cording. Tie the loose ends to a tassel for a decorative touch.

Attach an awning cleat to the window frame and wrap the cording around the cleat to secure the shade at various heights.

▲ *Cording pulled through the loops in Roman shade tape allows the shade to be adjusted to any height. Firmly woven fabrics, such as canvas, work best for this type of shade.*

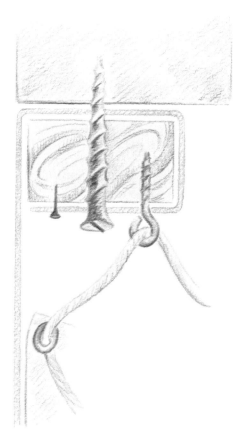

▲ Lightweight fabric and contrasting ties make an elegant shade. The ties form neat bows at the bottom of the shade.

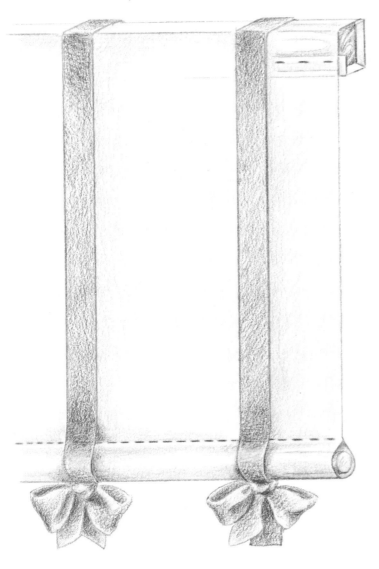

Tied Shade

Cut the shade fabric and lining 2 inches wider and 8 inches longer than the desired size of the finished shade. With right sides together, stitch 1 inch from the side and bottom edges. Turn right side out and press.

Turn the bottom edge toward the lining to make a 1½-inch casing. Stitch along the top edge of the casing.

Place a strip of lattice or 1- x 2-inch wood (1½ inches shorter than the finished width of the shade) at the top of the shade. Staple the top edge of the shade to the lattice. Wrap the top of the shade once around the lattice, as shown in the diagram.

To make the ties for the shade, cut eight 5-inch-wide strips of fabric, each 12 inches longer than the finished shade. Place the right sides of two strips of fabric together and stitch a 1-inch seam from the side and bottom edges. Sew the other pairs of strips together in the same way. Turn each tie right side out and press. (Ties can also be made from 3-inch-wide ribbon.)

Place one tie on each side of the front of the shade, about 6 inches from the side edge. Fold the raw edge of each tie under and staple the end to the lattice strip. Staple another tie to the same spot, letting the ties hang down the back of the shade. Nail the lattice strip either above the window frame or inside it.

To weight the bottom of the shade, use a 1-inch diameter wooden dowel or a strip of lattice that is 2 inches shorter than the finished width of the shade. Insert the dowel into the casing. Roll the shade up to the desired height and tie the front and back ties together at the bottom of the shade, forming either a knot or a bow. Long ties can be gathered into plump bows at the bottom of the shade. As an alternative to using a wooden dowel to weight the shade, simply roll or gather the fabric into soft folds for a luxurious look.

No-Sew Window Treatments

Fabric Knot

To fashion a big decorative knot for a no-sew window treatment, fold fabric around a length of cotton batting or polyester stuffing to form a tube. Secure the ends of the tube with rubber bands as shown in the diagram.

Loosely knot the tube of fabric around your wrist; tie a second knot around your wrist close to the first one.

With the same hand, grasp the long, loose tube of fabric; slide the double knot off of your wrist, pulling a loop of the tube into the center, as shown. To complete the knot, fasten both tubes off with rubber bands close to the base of the knot. Hang the knot on a nail at the corner of the window frame.

▲ *Positioning the knot on a nail hides the heading of the draperies.*

◄ *The large fabric knot is tied from fabric made plump with polyester stuffing.*

Pouf Swag

Cut a fabric panel 25 inches deep and 3 times the width of the window. Make a deep box pleat in the center of the panel. Each half of the pleat should be 10 inches deep. Pin at the top to secure as shown in the diagram.

Gather the fabric vertically at the center of the box pleat, as shown. Secure the gathers with a string. Finger-pleat the fabric horizontally on either side at the points indicated by dotted lines on the diagram. Tie the pleats with string to secure them.

Tie the pouf to the rod, allowing it to sag gracefully between the ties. Make self-fabric bows and pin them to the valance to conceal the ties.

▲ *Self-fabric bows pinned to the valance conceal the ties to the curtain rod.*

Bow-Tied Swag

Using fabric glue or fusible fabric strips, seam two pieces of fabric together lengthwise to make a panel 60 inches deep and 2½ times the desired width of the valance. Fold the panel in half along the seam to make a lined panel. Fold 1 inch of fabric under on the top edges. Clip the top edges together with clothespins at evenly spaced intervals, shown as points A through E in the diagram.

With pins, mark B1 and D1 on the seam line directly below B and D. Gather B1 and D1 up to join with B and D. Secure with clothespins already holding B and D. Arrange the valance on the rod so that the clothespins are evenly spaced, allowing the panel to drop gracefully between the pins.

To complete the valance, make oversize bows from fabric scraps. Use a hot-glue gun to attach the bows to the clothespins. Replace the plain clothespins on the rod with the bowed clothespins.

▲ *The swag is clipped to the rod with clothespins.*

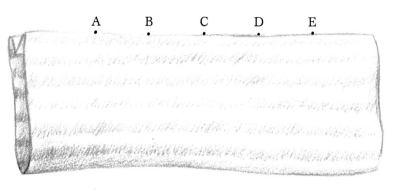

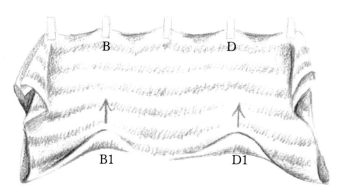

▲ *Oversize bows are glued to clothespins to conceal the mechanics of attaching the swag.*

Easy-Sew Swag

A simple, one-piece swag can be made by cutting fabric the width of the window plus 8 inches. To determine the length, simply add 4 inches to the desired finished length of the swag. To give the swag body, line it with cotton lining fabric cut to the same dimensions.

To make the ruffle, cut strips of fabric, each 5-inches wide. Stitch the short ends of the fabric together to make one long strip. You will need a strip of fabric approximately 6 times the window width. Fold the strip of fabric in half lengthwise and press to form a strip 2½ inches deep. Make a gathering stitch ½ inch from the raw edge and gather. The finished ruffle should measure half the length of the ungathered strip.

Place the swag fabric and the lining with right sides together. Pin the gathered ruffle between the two layers along the sides and bottom, with the folded edge of the ruffle toward the center of the swag. Stitch ½ inch from the raw edge along the sides and bottom of the swag. Turn the swag right side out and press.

Turn the top of the swag under ¼ inch and press. Then turn under 1½ inches and stitch to make a 1½-inch casing for the curtain rod.

Cut two strips of Roman shade tape to fit from the bottom seam of the swag to the bottom of the casing, allowing approximately ¼ inch on each end for seam allowances and adjusting the tape so that the lower ring of each strip of tape is 1 inch from the bottom seam of the swag (1 inch above the top of the ruffle). Turn under ¼ inch at the top

▲ *A charming ruffled swag is paired with crisp, white window shutters for privacy.*

and at the bottom edge of the tape. Machine-stitch the tape to the back of the swag, stitching through both layers of fabric.

Run Roman shade cord or lightweight traverse cord through the rings on each strip of tape. Insert the curtain rod in the casing and hang the swag. Pull the cording up on each side to raise the swag to the desired height. Tie the upper ends of the cording to the top rings of the Roman shade tape and trim the excess cording.

Braided Edging

A special handmade braid can add drama to a window treatment or detail to a pillow. It can be made from lightweight fabrics that either match or contrast with your draperies or pillows.

To make the braided edging, cut three different fabric strips 4 times as wide as you want the finished strip to be (approximately ⅓ the finished width of the braided trim). Fold the edges of the fabric strip in evenly toward the center as shown in the diagram; then fold the strip in half and press. Tie the three strips together or secure with a rubber band and braid. Sew the finished edging to your curtain or pillow by hand.

▲ *Braided edging adds drama to any window treatment.*

▲ *Two solid-color strips and one patterned strip of fabric braided together add exquisite detail to draperies.*

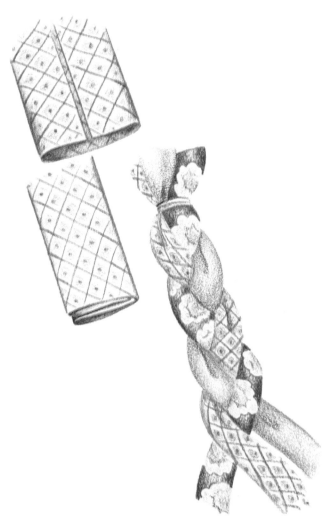

172

Floors

Painted Floors

A smooth surface is very important when painting a floor, so be sure that all of the old finish has been removed before you begin. After the finish is removed, sand the floor with fine sandpaper. It also helps to sand lightly between coats of paint to smooth the surface for the next coat. Painting with an initial coat of primer will help the paint go on more smoothly.

Most types of paint are suitable for use on floors. Latex paint is especially easy to use, since it cleans up with water. Oil-base paint is very durable and cleans up easily with turpentine or mineral spirits. Protect the painted finish with a final coat of clear polyurethane varnish.

Checkerboard Floor

To paint a checkerboard floor, begin by painting the entire floor the lightest color to be used in the design; sand between coats and allow the floor to dry completely before proceeding to the next step.

Determine the center of the area to be painted and start measuring your design there. To make the checkerboard pattern, use masking tape to mark off the squares. The floor pictured in Chapter II was laid out in 12-inch-square blocks. You may choose to make the blocks smaller or larger, depending on the size of the area to be painted. After marking off the squares, paint alternate blocks using the second, darker color of paint. When the floor has dried completely, apply at least two coats of clear polyurethane varnish to protect the painted surface.

Inlay Floor

You can combine several painting techniques, such as marbling, stenciling, lightening, and staining, to give wood floors the look of inlay. An inlay pattern of light and dark woods is especially useful in a hallway where you need a graceful link between one room with a light floor and another where the floor is dark. An inlay pattern can also be used to create a special border around an area rug. You might also use just a touch of painted inlay in a doorway as a way of creating a special entrance to a large room.

Before you get out the paint, draw your floor

▲ *Light and dark finishes in a hallway painted in an inlay design create a smooth transition from dark wood floors in one area of the house to lightened floors at the other end.*

▲ *Squares of richly veined green faux marble join the alternating light and dark wood octagons. A classic medallion motif spans the marbleized threshold. (Instructions for painting a faux finish are in this chapter.)*

space to scale on graph paper and plan the placement of the inlay design. Simple patterns, such as checkerboards or free-form designs, are good for a beginning project. Decide which areas of the pattern are to be light, which are to be dark, and which will have a painted finish.

Using a pencil and a yardstick, draw the inlay pattern on the floor. Most inlay patterns are composed of light areas (which are lightened with diluted white paint), dark areas (which are stained), and painted areas. Begin by brushing diluted white paint on the lightest areas of your design. Apply wood stain to the darkest areas. Use a small brush to apply paint to the painted areas. You may even want to top your design with a stencil, but be sure that the paint has dried completely before stenciling.

Use a black permanent-ink marker to draw lines between the different colors. When the inlay design is completely dry, finish the floor with at least two coats of clear polyurethane varnish.

Pickled Floor

Many existing hardwood floors are oak, a relatively light wood that is appropriate for pickling. Other wood floors, such as pine, can also be easily pickled.

It is a good idea to get professional help to sand your floors to prepare them for pickling. You can

▲ *A pickled look is achieved in a two-step process: white enamel thinned slightly with mineral spirits is brushed on and immediately wiped off with a clean cloth. The lighter floor brightens the entire room.*

rent electric floor sanders, but they are difficult to use without experience, and you could damage your floors.

Lightening floors yourself is an ambitious project, but one that can be safely tackled once the floors are sanded. Work first on a test area that will be covered later by a rug or a piece of furniture. An even application is most important and is best achieved with one person working to complete the job in a single day.

Brush white enamel paint thinned with mineral spirits onto the raw wood, then wipe away the excess to achieve the desired effect. If you have help, have one person brush on the solution and the other wipe it away. Since the paint solution penetrates deeper along the softer grain lines, lightening also has the effect of intensifying the wood's natural grain pattern.

Vacuum the floor and dust with a clean, slightly damp cloth before applying clear polyurethane varnish. Apply two coats, adding a third coat to pine floors, since they are susceptible to dents.

Floorcoverings

▲ Adding a stenciled floorcloth is an easy way to give your room a fresh, seasonal look.

Stenciled Floorcloth

To make a floorcloth, purchase heavy cotton canvas from an awning company or art supply store. Turn 1 to 4 inches of canvas to the underside and secure with white glue, fusible material, or a hot-glue gun.

To make the floorcloth flat, waterproof, and durable, you will need to size it. Mix a solution of one part gesso (purchased at an art supply store), one part white glue, and one part water. If the solution thickens, thin it with water. With a stiff brush, coat one side of the canvas. Let it dry, then repeat on the other side.

Use artists' acrylic polymer paints or enamels to paint the canvas. Draw the design lightly in pencil and fill in with paint. You can also use stencils to create a pattern on the floorcloth.

To protect the painted floorcloth, apply three coats of polyurethane varnish or acrylic polymer varnish. Polyurethane will darken the canvas but will be quite durable. Acrylic polymer varnish is non-yellowing. Either finish can be cleaned with soap and water.

Use cloth carpet tape to secure a floorcloth to the floor. The tape should be placed on the underside of the floorcloth and fastened to all four sides, flush with the edges. Placing a thin rubber pad underneath will keep the floorcloth from slipping and will also increase its durability.

175

Painted Sisal Rug

A combination of stenciling and hand painting can be used to create a stunning design for a sisal rug. All you need to begin is a paintbrush and acrylic paints.

To paint bands of color on your rug, use masking tape to mark the desired widths on the rug. Paint in the bands, using acrylic paint.

For a leaf design, you can copy fabric or trace leaves taken from garden plants or books. Cut a stencil for your design, using the instructions for making stencils given in Stenciled Walls. A pointed paintbrush works well to add shading to leaf designs and to paint colorful floral accents. For a freehand design, draw the design lightly with a pencil, then paint.

A small design such as a flower or leaf, stenciled at intervals across the rug, adds interesting detail.

▲ *An elaborate bow is painted freehand to match a bedroom's frilly decor.*

▲ *Flowing lines and shaded colors enhance a simple border design.*

176

Fabric-Dyed Rug

You can turn a simple woven sisal rug into a hand-painted treasure just by applying fabric dye to the pattern already woven into the rug. Use the rug's woven pattern as a guide in determining your design. The finished piece will resemble a geometric quilt.

Powdered fabric dyes and liquid concentrates work equally well for painting a sisal rug. Use the concentrate straight from the bottle or dilute it with water to lighten the color. The shade of the powdered dye is determined by the amount of water added. Try the dyes on a test square to check the intensity of the color.

Using the weave of the rug as a guide, paint the design with a ½-inch flat brush. It is easier to paint all of one color first, then paint the second color. If you make a mistake, quickly blot it with a paper towel. Painting over an area more than once will darken the color.

After the rug has dried completely, spray it with a coat or two of clear polyurethane to protect the painted design.

▲ *Both powdered fabric dye and liquid concentrate can be used to paint a straw rug. Buy a few extra squares of the rug material and practice applying the dye before actually painting the rug.*

▲ *A rag rug is made from strips cut from bed sheets.*

Crocheted Rag Rug

To crochet a 60- x 30-inch rag rug (including fringe), you will need 4 double-bed flat sheets (or 24 yards of 48- or 54-inch-wide fabric). Cut the fabric lengthwise in ½-inch-wide strips.

Row 1: With a size N crochet hook, crochet a chain 48 inches long, leaving a 6-inch tail unworked at the beginning of the strip to form the fringe. Fasten off at the end of the chain and cut the strip, leaving a 6-inch tail at the end.

Row 2: Join on at the beginning of the previously worked chain, leaving a 6-inch tail of new strip unworked, and work 1 single crochet in each chain of the previous row. Fasten off at the end, leaving a 6-inch tail. For remaining rows, work even in single crochet until the rug is 30 inches wide, leaving 6-inch strips unworked at the beginning and end of each row.

To approximate the color proportions of the rug pictured in Chapter I, use 50% light green, 25% pink, and 25% print strips (2 light green sheets, 1 pink sheet, and 1 large-scale floral print sheet), joining on new colors as desired to produce a random effect. Knot the strips together to join, pulling the ends of the strips to the wrong side of the rug when finished.

When the rug is completed, spray it lightly with water to dampen, and block it to the desired dimensions, fastening it in place on the blocking surface with T-pins. Allow to dry before unpinning the rug.

Stenciled Rag Rug

Stenciling a rag rug is a fast, fun way to give it new personality. Even old rugs will seem like new when you stencil them with bright colors and lively designs.

Because a rag rug consists of many rows of cotton with rows of space between, a large stencil design works best; small designs tend to get lost in the spaces. Whether you draw your own design or use a precut stencil, you may need to adjust the size of the pattern to fit the scale of your rug. Instructions for making stencils are in the section on stenciled walls.

Use either acrylic paint or fabric dye to paint the rug. Acrylic paint sits on top of the rug and hardens, while fabric dye penetrates the cloth and remains soft. So for a high-traffic area, fabric dye may be preferable, since it is more resilient.

Use a round stencil brush with even-length bristles for painting on a rag rug; you can dab paint into the crevices and under the threads of the fabric without smearing it under your stencil. As with any stenciling, clean the stencil frequently to avoid staining the fabric or blurring the painted design.

Heat-set the paint or dye using an iron and pressing cloth. After the design has been heat-set, you can follow the normal washing instructions for your rug.

▲ *A single, large-scale stencil gives new personality to a rag rug. Size and color selection help produce a weather-vane design with a contemporary look.*

Furniture

Hand-Painted Furniture

Faux Marble

You can marble almost any surface to which paint will adhere — wood, metal, wallboard, and unglazed ceramics. Marbling is easy, and with a faux marble finish, you have a wider range of colors than with real marble.

The real joy of this marbling technique, though, is that it is infallible. You can smudge, sand, or paint out any area that does not please you. Glaze over colors that are too bold; add veins with a brush; or emphasize details with a marker — in short, play with the paint until you get the effect you like. That effect can be either subtle or bold, whatever suits you.

For the base coat, select latex paint in a shade that will be the background color for the finished project. You will also need acrylic paint and marker pens in various colors of your choice to complete your design.

Use a disposable pie tin as a palette. With a puddle of latex paint in the center and dime-sized drops of acrylic accent colors on either side, drag a 3- or 4-inch brush or sponge applicator through the palette, just tipping the edges of the brush or sponge in the accent colors. Test your strokes on newspaper, twisting the brush to gently mingle accent colors with latex. To apply to the furniture surface, brush diagonally from left to right in a wavy motion. Repeat parallel strokes until the entire surface is covered.

While the paint is wet, use a finger or damp sponge to smudge any color that is too solid. A few dramatic streaks in strategic places can be very effective. To add veins of pure color, dip the side of your brush in an accent color and apply it in a wavy line. Add accents of deeper color with a marker pen.

If your colors are too bold after the design has dried, use cheesecloth to wipe on a glaze of diluted latex paint. Wipe away any excess, leaving a transparent film. If at any point you do not like the effect, simply paint over it with latex and try again.

▲ *The secret to imitating marble lies in the way you load the brush and make wavy diagonal strokes.*

Colorful Details

Nothing brings individuality to a room like a piece of hand-painted furniture. With carefully chosen vintage furniture and a refreshing selection of colors, you can add a bright stroke of originality to any room in your home.

Painted pieces blend with any decor. A treasure found in a second-hand store or even the attic can be updated with new shades, and the colors can be planned to help blend an older style with existing furnishings. A new, unfinished table or chair, when painted, can add a lively dash of color to an otherwise neutral setting.

The most fashionable painted pieces are rarely a single, solid color. Instead, several subtly different hues highlight the shape or decorations of the piece. When selecting furniture to paint, look for interesting details, such as curved moldings or carvings.

When considering colors, plan the painted piece as a complementary accent in the room rather than as a showstopper in itself. Choose a mellow base color to blend with or echo the room's dominant tone. Against this subtle background, you can reflect the room's accent colors in the piece's small details.

▲ *The inside edges of the arms are painted a different color from the outer edges.*

◄ *Cotton-candy pastels add a romantic touch to a chair.*

The first step is choosing a piece of furniture with smooth wood, uncracked from age or exposure. The wood must be stripped clean of all dirt, oil, and old paint. Be thorough at this step. Any overlooked patch will be magnified by the new coat of paint.

To create a soft, semitransparent background color, thin oil-base paint in a ratio of 2 parts paint to 1 part mineral spirits. Use a 2- or 2½-inch brush. Keep plenty of soft, lint-free cotton cloths nearby to rub away excess paint.

Let the piece dry overnight before painting in the details. If your accent touches follow straight lines, use masking tape as a guide. Just remember to remove it a few hours after painting. For glossy, opaque highlights, apply oil-base paint at full strength, using a small pointed brush.

▲ *Ribbons of gold and red highlight the turned legs and rippled top of an old table, coated in a muted green.*

▲ *A colorful hand-painted finish adds new life to vintage furniture.*

Milk Paint

Milk paint (a mixture of equal parts milk, lime, and pigment) creates a durable, matte finish with a centuries-old look. With milk paint, you can give an authentic folk-art finish to a new piece of furniture or to one you may be restoring.

The rich colors of milk paint can add real life to a room when applied to a large piece of furniture. You can also use milk paint on small wooden accessories, such as Shaker boxes and trays. Painting small objects is a good way to try your hand at mixing paint, estimating coverage, and combining colors.

You can use powdered milk paint that is available commercially, or you can mix your own supply. As with any water-based coloring, milk paint adheres best when applied to raw wood. If you are refinishing a piece and prefer not to strip it first, at least sand the surface thoroughly before painting. The first coat of milk paint can serve as the primer. Allow at least four hours drying time before adding the second coat, which deepens the coloring.

▶ *The rich colors of milk paint enliven a room when applied to a large piece of furniture. Rubbing the surface of the piece with linseed or tung oil is an easy way to deepen the final color and also to help seal and protect the finish.*

Recipe for Milk Paint
Coverage with milk paint is a bit less dense than for most paints. A batch with two ounces each of milk, lime, and coloring should be enough to cover a coffee table or ladder-back chair.

Combine one part milk (either skim milk, buttermilk, or dehydrated milk powder or crystals); one part lime; and one part coloring (powdered tempera paint or paint colorants, available at art supply stores). After mixing the three ingredients, strain through cheesecloth to rid the mixture of lumps.

While the paint is wet, you can clean your brushes and pan with soap and water. Once it dries, it is there to stay.

For a look that is especially authentic, apply two different colors, such as red over black. A build-up of layers is common with early painted furniture because the first coloring was usually not stripped before repainting the piece.

With a little sanding of key areas after the paint has dried, you can lend an aged look to the furniture. Sand in the direction of the wood grain to reveal some of the bottom layer of color and to add natural character lines. Concentrate sanding in areas that would ordinarily receive more wear over time, such as knobs, edges, and corners.

You can make the look even more authentic by lightly rubbing the entire surface with fine-grained sandpaper. Wear a face mask as protection against the lime in the paint dust and work in a well-ventilated area. Wipe the surfaces with a damp cloth to remove dust particles. You may want to apply a coat of linseed or tung oil as a final coat to give the finish a softer look and to darken it.

▶ *The key to the authentic folk-art look of milk-painted furniture is to simulate age by sanding certain areas that would receive more wear, such as corners and knobs.*

▼ *Small projects are a fun way to test milk paint colors and painting techniques.*

Stenciled Furniture

A little stenciling adds a stylish touch to an old piece of painted or stained furniture.

You can stencil chair seats, the top or apron of a table, cabinet doors, drawer fronts, or any other suitable area on your furniture. The finish on the piece you select by no means must be perfect, but you should remove excess wax before beginning so that the paint will adhere.

Books of precut stencils are readily available, but if you want an original look, you can create your own design and make a stencil. A good way to coordinate the stenciled pattern with the room's furnishings is to copy the design from the fabric or wallpaper used in the room. If you select a design from fabric or wallpaper to use as your motif, spread the fabric or wallpaper out on a table. Examine the design to find the one element that seems most characteristic. Try to visualize this element repeated several times. For ease in stenciling, the design you copy should be a manageable size, approximately 7 inches square.

Place a piece of tracing paper over the design. Trace the main shapes, keeping them simple. The shapes should be individual and should not overlap or touch. (For a good illustration of how a flower motif from fabric might be adapted to a stencil design, see page 185.)

Place a piece of acetate over the traced design. Cut a separate stencil for each color you are planning to use. For example, a design with two colors will require two stencils, and so on. (As an alternative, use one stencil and cover the open areas not being painted with masking tape.) Using a sharp craft knife, cut away only those areas of the design that will be of one color. Work on a cutting board, keep a firm pressure on the knife, try to make one continuous cut, and be sure cuts at the corners are clean. To hold the stencil together, leave narrow strips of acetate between the openings.

Use the stencils in sequence. When the first color has dried, overlay the next stencil and apply the second color. (When using one stencil for all of the colors, mask off with tape the colors not being painted at that time, then paint the open areas of the design.)

To stencil, position the stencil on the surface to be painted. Use masking tape to help hold the stencil pattern in place. With your fingertip or a stencil brush, dab light layers of artists' acrylic paint (either in jars or tubes) through the openings in the design. Continue to apply the paint until you have filled in all the design openings. Clean the front and back edges of the stencils frequently.

▲ *Designs were traced from a book of botanical prints to create stencils in keeping with the garden look of the room.*

▲ *Acrylic paint creates soft layers of color. The panels of the door act as frames for the stenciled flowers.*

When the paint is dry, apply a thin coat of clear acrylic spray to seal the design. Your stenciled design will last a long time, but take care not to apply furniture polish directly to the painted area.

Fabric-Dyed Furniture

Fabric dye, like stain, lets the natural beauty of the wood grain show through. Since each piece of wood absorbs the dye a little differently, depending on its grain, be ready for surprises. Effects can range from pastel tints to deeply saturated tones. However the grain responds, the results will be highly individual and will add a colorful accent to your room.

You can apply a solid coat of fabric dye to your furniture, or you may choose to enhance the dyed piece by using the technique described after this section for stenciling with spray varnish.

The fabric dye method works only on bare wood furniture that has never been painted or varnished. A liquid concentrate form of fabric dye is available, which may be used just as it comes from the bottle, or it can be diluted slightly with water.

The fabric dye color deepens considerably as it dries. When a coat of varnish is applied to the finished piece (as it must be, to prevent the dye from rubbing off), the colors will have a richer appearance. Test all colors in an inconspicuous place on the furniture before beginning your project and check the color only after it has dried completely.

You can use a brush to apply the fabric dye, but some interesting effects can also be achieved by sponging the surface with the dye. Water-base dye tends to bleed, especially on very porous wood, so avoid any pattern that requires a hard, crisp edge.

A misty watercolor effect can be achieved by wetting the wood with water before applying the dye. This also tends to lighten the color. Apply dye in the direction of the wood grain and take care to avoid the streaky look that comes from overlapping brush marks. If streaks are too noticeable, brush another coat of dye over the entire area.

If you make a mistake that cannot be covered with another color, bleach it out and start again. Mix liquid bleach with a small amount of water and brush it on the wood. Rinse the brush promptly. When the mistake has faded, rub with a damp cloth to remove as much bleach as possible; then allow the surface to dry completely before applying the dye again.

Allow the dyed surfaces to dry overnight; then sand and apply a protective coat of clear varnish. For best results, use at least two coats of varnish. Allow the first coat to dry, sand it lightly, and wipe off any dust; then apply the final coat.

Stenciling with Varnish

To combine stenciled designs with the fabric dye technique described in the preceding section, begin with the stenciling on the bare wood. Position your stencil pattern on the unfinished surface of the piece to be stenciled. Use masking tape to hold the stencil in place. Mask other surface areas with newspaper. Spray three light coats of clear varnish through the stencil, allowing each coat of varnish to dry before applying the next. Continue until you complete the entire stencil design.

After the varnish has dried, paint the piece with fabric dye following the guidelines above. The varnish will act as a resist when the dye is brushed on the surface, leaving the stenciled design intact.

▲ *Three coats of varnish, sprayed through a graceful tulip stencil, act as a resist when fabric dye is brushed on the rest of the chair.*

Light Wood Finishes

Light wood finishes are a signature of the casual country look in decorating. Because of their versatility, light woods also blend well with contemporary furnishings. Pickling and bleaching are two of the easiest methods of lightening wood.

Before wood furniture can be bleached, it must be paint free, dirt free, and dry. Remove all hardware and completely strip any finishes, then sand the surface lightly to open up the wood's pores. Wiping down the wood with lacquer thinner will also open the pores, which in turn helps the bleach to penetrate.

Pickling

A pickled look, or lightening effect, can be applied over any light wood (either naturally light or bleached). The method is just as easy and costs no more than staining or painting furniture.

Working on one section at a time, brush on white enamel paint that has been thinned slightly with mineral spirits. Let the paint settle in nicks, cracks, and recessed areas. Then immediately wipe off the paint with a clean cloth, leaving some paint behind in hard-to-reach areas. When the paint has completely dried, replace the hardware that was removed (or add your own white porcelain knobs or brass pulls). Buff the furniture with light-toned wood wax to protect the finish.

Bleaching

Although several products can be used to bleach wood, liquid household bleach seems to be the favorite among professional refinishers. This product offers several advantages: it is easy to find, usually requires no mixing, and is less likely to raise the grain than commercial wood bleaches. Any brand will do the job as long as it contains sodium hypochlorite. Simply cover furniture surfaces with full-strength liquid bleach, using a cloth or sponge, and allow to dry naturally.

Another bleaching product, oxalic acid, is available at most paint and hardware stores in crystallized form and must be dissolved in warm water. Oxalic acid is best used for removing color from stain that has soaked into the wood and remains after the furniture is stripped. Apply oxalic acid with a brush and continue to apply the solution, to keep the wood moist, for about a half hour before allowing it to dry. It may then be necessary to buff the wood with grade 0 steel wool.

A third bleaching product, also available at paint and hardware stores, consists of two liquid chemicals packaged separately, sodium hydroxide and hydrogen peroxide. This powerful solution must be thoroughly rinsed off when it has dried, to remove the salt residue. Again, it may be necessary to rub the dried surface with steel wool.

On any bleaching project, protect yourself from caustic fumes by working in a well-ventilated area, wearing rubber gloves, and following package instructions carefully. Always use glass or plastic containers, since acid often reacts with metal.

Little change in color will be noticeable while the wood is wet. If the piece is still too dark after it has dried (generally after four hours or so) repeat the bleaching process until you get the desired shade. Placing the furniture in direct sunlight can help speed the drying process and may even encourage the effects of the bleach. Allow the wood to dry completely (twenty-four hours if possible) before applying wax or other protective coatings.

▲ *After stripping, an antique heart-pine table required nothing more than a natural wax finish to enhance its mellow patina. A pickled-look finish was applied to a chair, which blends well with the table and pickled floor.*

Pierced-Tin Panels

Anyone who has ever admired an antique pie safe thinks about doing something with pierced tin. When used as panels for cabinet doors, pierced tin gives any kitchen an authentic country look.

You can have a carpenter build door frames to hold the tin. Or if you already have wall cabinets with recessed panels in the doors, you can attach the pierced tin directly to the wood panel.

If you are working with open frames, to get the measurements for the tin panel, measure the opening in each frame and add 2 inches to both the length and width. If you already have wall cabinets with wood-panel doors, measure the length and width of the wood panel inside the door frame.

Cut out each tin panel with tin snips. Cut a piece of paper the same size as the panel and draw your pattern on the paper. Place the tin panel on a piece of scrap plywood and tape the pattern over the tin.

To punch the design, use a variety of nails for different-sized round cuts. Use screwdrivers of different sizes to punch slits. (Note: This use will damage screwdrivers. Use old ones or substitute a small cold chisel.) The size of the holes and slits depends on how hard you hammer the punching tool.

If you are working with new door frames, turn the rough edges of the tin toward the front of the design; then nail the pierced panel to the inside of the door frames. In this way, you will be less likely to brush against them as you reach inside the cabinets.

If you are applying a tin panel to an existing wood panel door, place the rough side of the tin against the wood. Drive small brads into the door frame at an angle to hold the tin in place.

Alternatives to tin are thin-gauged galvanized sheet metal and hobby aluminum. Neither has a finish as attractive as tin, but a coat of burnt umber glaze will reduce the shine and give an aged look.

Accessories

Tablecloths

Round Tablecloth

The width of a double-bed sheet gives you enough fabric to cut a round, floor-length tablecloth without seaming. Buy a double flat sheet to make a cloth up to 81 inches in diameter; a queen flat sheet for 82 to 90 inches; and a king flat sheet for a tablecloth 91 to 102 inches in diameter.

Fabric other than sheets is usually not wide enough to make a round tablecloth without seaming. You can, however, sew two or three lengths of fabric together to create the width of fabric needed. To get the measurement for the amount of fabric needed, measure the diameter of the tabletop plus twice the drop (distance from the table edge to the floor). Add 2 inches for the hem allowance. You will need enough fabric to seam together a square with sides equal to the diameter of the entire cloth plus the hem. (When stitching your panels of fabric together, be sure to avoid a center seam by using one full panel of fabric for the center panel of the cloth.)

Make a compass by tying a non-stretch string around a pencil. To determine the length of the string, divide the sum of the table measurements in half (tabletop measurement, plus twice the drop, plus the 2 inch hem, divided by 2).

Fold the sheet (or length of fabric) in half horizontally; then fold in half vertically. Tack the end of the compass string at the folded corner. Swing an arc as shown in the diagram. For accuracy, be sure to hold the pencil perpendicular to the sheet. Cut through all four layers of fabric along the penciled line. Turn under the raw edge 1 inch and machine-stitch the hem.

Round Tablecloth with Shirred Welt

Cut out a circle of fabric with a diameter 1 inch larger than the diameter of the tabletop. Cut a length of 1-inch cording equal to the circumference of the circle of fabric. Cut and seam together 6-inch-wide bias fabric strips to equal a length 2½ times the length of the cording. Shirr the pieced bias tube of fabric onto the cording, then machine-stitch the cording onto the circle.

Measure the drop to get the width for the skirt fabric. Add 1¼ inches to that measurement to accommodate seam allowances at the top and bottom of the skirt.

To determine the length of fabric needed for a full skirt, measure the circumference of the table; then double (or triple, for extra fullness) that measurement. Cut the fabric to the measured width; then seam together enough pieces of fabric to achieve the fullness desired.

Cut and seam together 6-inch-wide bias fabric strips to equal a length 2½ times the length of fabric needed for the skirt. Shirr the pieced bias tube of fabric onto 1-inch cording and machine-stitch to the bottom of the skirt.

Make ¾-inch-wide knife pleats in the skirt fabric, pressing the pleats as you go. Baste or pin the pleats. Sew the knife-pleated skirt to the shirred cording on the tabletop circle of fabric.

Flat, self-fabric bows may be tacked in place just under the top cording and slightly above the bottom cording.

▶ *Fabric shirred on 1-inch cording and a knife-pleated skirt add sophisticated style to a round tablecloth.*

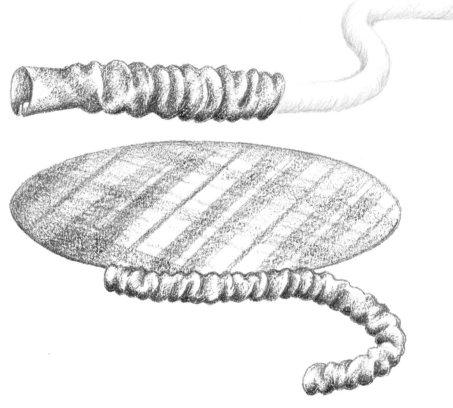

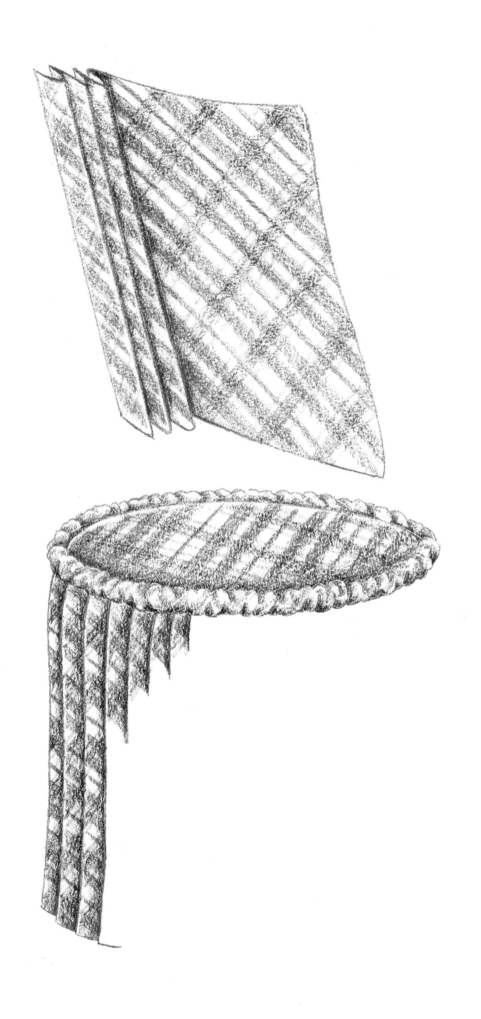

Square or Rectangular Tablecloth

To make a floor-length covering for a square or rectangular table, measure the tabletop. Cut a piece of fabric and a piece of lining 1 inch wider and longer than the measurements to allow for a ½-inch seam on all sides. With wrong sides together, baste the lining to the fabric on all four sides.

For the skirt, first measure the drop. Add 1½ inches to that measurement to allow for the hem; the lining should be 1½ inches shorter than the drop.

Measure all four table sides; add 20 inches to each measurement to allow for the pleats. Using these measurements, cut panels of fabric and lining for each side of the tablecloth.

Sew the four fabric panels together at the ends, right sides together, to form one long rectangle. Press seams open. Repeat with the lining.

Align the lining with the fabric rectangle, right sides together. Stitch at hem, using a ½-inch seam allowance. Press seams open; turn right side out. Baste the fabric rectangle and the lining together at the open end. Press the hem formed at the bottom.

Starting at one end of the rectangular drop panel, measure in 10 inches; at this point, begin pinning the drop panel to the tabletop piece, right sides together. Stop pinning at the first corner of the tabletop piece, leaving another 10 inches of excess fabric. Bring the seam of the drop panel to the corner of the tabletop piece. Pin temporarily. Leaving another 10 inches of fabric loose after the seam, continue pinning along the remaining three sides of the tabletop piece, treating the corners as described above.

Using the 10 inches of excess fabric at each side of the corners (a total of 20 inches of excess fabric at each corner), fold two 5-inch pleats. (Each 5-inch pleat requires 10 inches of fabric.) See the diagram. Bring the folds together at the seam and press flat. Pin to the tabletop piece. Remove the temporary pin at the corner. Notch the corners of the drop panel to allow for 90-degree turns. Sew along the length of the drop panel, incorporating the pleats at the corners. Repeat with the other lengths.

Make fabric bows; attach them with Velcro strips.

▲ *A floor-length covering for a square or rectangular table is only slightly more involved to sew than a round skirt. Generous pleats at each corner add the fullness needed for guests to slide their chairs under the table.*

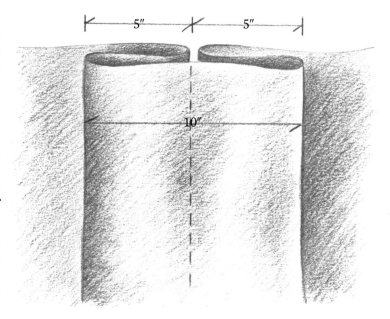

Simple Pillows

Tied Pillow Covers

Slipcover tired pillows by using fabrics you have around the house. Lacy table runners, colorful dinner napkins, and even stylish silk scarves can be pressed into service to give your pillows new life. You can quickly change your pillows for the holidays or coordinate them with a special table setting, and these makeovers do not require sewing, cutting, or gluing. Simple knots, ribbons, and pins from your jewelry box keep the covers in place.

The easiest method is to tie a table runner around a pillow and square-knot it in the front. Tuck the ends into the knot and secure them with safety pins where necessary.

Using napkins is another simple way to slipcover pillows. Sandwich a pillow between two dinner napkins and secure the four corners with rubber bands. Finger-crease a pleat in the edges to create a neat flange; then cover the rubber bands with bow-tied ribbons. Place mats, handkerchiefs, bandannas, and washcloths or hand towels are possibilities for this method. Just make sure that the cloths are large enough to cover the pillow completely, and that the ties are appropriate to the mood of the fabric. For example, jute string would be a rugged counterpart for tying a bandanna-covered pillow; ropes of plastic seed pearls would be a fitting way to tie a pillow covered with lacy handkerchiefs.

The way you secure a scarf depends on the size of the scarf in relation to the size of the pillow. If the ends of the scarf are too short to knot, simply hold them in place with a rubber band. Then spread the ends in a neat, symmetrical arrangement. Medium-long edges can be folded into a rosette. After securing with a rubber band, stuff three corners of the scarf under the fourth; arrange the fourth so it forms a pouf over them. Keep the pouf in place with another rubber band, then poke the center inside the rubber band.

However you finish the pillow, if you do not like the way the knot looks, turn the pillow over. Pillows wrapped with scarves have smooth bias backs that look great on their own.

▼ *Two pastel dinner napkins cover a small pillow for a demure look. Ribbon ties at each corner camouflage the rubber bands that hold the cover in place.*

◄Scarves put pizzazz into plain pillows. A square scarf of striped silk knots over a small pillow for easy elegance. The larger pillow was tied with a bright paisley scarf and the knot turned to the back.

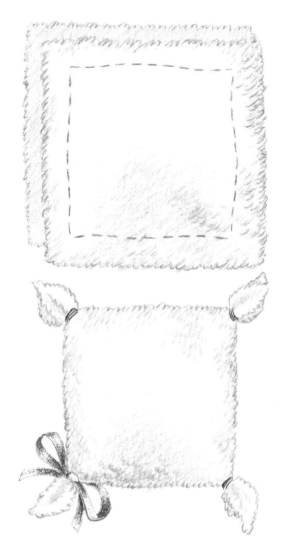

Use antique dresser scarves and table runners, long fashion scarves, and wide woven belts for the simplest wraps. Tie in a square knot. Tuck ends back into the knot and secure with safety pins, if necessary. Add an antique brooch or silk flower.

Sandwich pillow form between two napkins, quilted place mats, bandannas, or terry cloth towels. Secure corners with rubber bands, then tie ribbon bows over the bands. Tuck edges of one napkin back inside the other napkin.

Pull all corners to the center and secure with a rubber band. Spread the ends in a neat, symmetrical arrangement. Longer ends can be tucked into a rosette, or each end can be twisted and wrapped to the back.

▲ *Pillows with knotted cording become important decorative accents in a room.*

Fancy Knotted Pillows

Knotted cording adds a distinctive touch to the most simple pillow, and the effect is easily accomplished. You simply cut two lengths of cording, cover them with fabric, and tie a simple knot, leaving long ends free to sew into the seam allowance of the pillow.

You can twist and knot the fabric-covered cording any way you like. Add fetching detail to a canvas pillow by featuring a nautical knot. Delicately twist cording covered in a contrasting fabric or color to make a pillow an important accent piece in a room. Or tie a masculine square knot to trim pillows in a den or young man's room.

Fabric strips for covering the cording should be cut on the bias to wrap smoothly around the cording. To determine how wide the fabric strip should be, add 1¼ inch to the circumference of the cording. (Find the circumference of the cording by wrapping a tape measure loosely around it.) Cut and piece the bias strips to form one long tube of fabric for each length of cording. Cover the cording with the pieced fabric strip. Tie the two lengths of cording into the desired knot, leaving enough cording to sew in with the seam allowance of the pillow. (If you use large cording, you may want to push the fabric strip back and cut the cording just short of the seam line; leaving only the fabric to be sewn into the seam.)

▲ *Create a series of designs from a single theme. Take one element, such as the top of the lily design, and repeat it in different ways. Add leaves, stems, and other simple shapes to vary the pattern.*

Painted Quilt-Block Pillows

Quilt-block pillows are an easy, colorful way to soften a chair or add a creative touch to a room. The graphic quality of quilt designs gives them a contemporary appeal that is right for many types of rooms. However, the process of actually cutting, piecing, and quilting a block takes a good bit of time. You may also be reluctant to cut even a damaged quilt into pillows. You can take a creative shortcut by using silk-technique fabric paints to make colorful and decorative "quilt" blocks to sew into pillows. You can paint your favorite quilt pattern, or you may want to try the design shown in the diagram, an adaptation of a favorite quilt called the Carolina Lily.

Silk-technique fabric paints are easy to apply and flow on smoothly. They are available in art supply stores. The paints can be blended to make many shades and diluted with water to make pastels. Silk paints differ from other fabric paints in that a clear liquid resist outlines each shape to keep the paint from spreading. These water-base paints are set with heat. You can use silk paints on fine cotton, silk, and most synthetics.

To paint a quilt block, draw the design directly onto fabric, using light pencil lines. Plan your design so that each separate area of color is a closed shape, such as a circle or an ellipse, and not an open shape, such as a *U*. Outline the design

with the resist, holding the tube like a pencil and following the pencil lines. Let the resist dry. Use a soft brush to apply the silk-technique paint inside the outlines. If you should accidentally apply the paint to an open shape, it will gradually spread out beyond the boundaries of the shape.

Set the painted design by ironing the fabric on the wrong side for a minute or two at a temperature suitable for the fabric. You can leave the resist lines in the fabric, or they can be removed by soaking the fabric in lukewarm water. When dry, the fabric is ready to be made into pillows.

◄ *You can adapt almost any quilt pattern and use it for painting pillows. For a coordinated look, repeat the color of your chair or sofa on one of the pillows.*

Stylish Bedspreads

Bedspread from Sheets

An easy way to make a lightweight summertime bedspread is to stitch two matching flat sheets together, using one for the top and one for the lining. Trim the selvage edges and open the hems of the sheets. Press the sheets and place them right sides together. Then stitch around three sides, leaving the bottom open. Turn the sheets right side out and press the seams. Turn the open seam to the inside, then sew by machine or by hand. At regular intervals over the surface of the bedspread, use a needle and thread to tack the two layers of fabric together.

The bedspread works best when made of dark-colored sheets. To determine if a patterned sheet with a light background is opaque enough to use, place two thicknesses of the sheet wrong sides together to see if the pattern of the sheet underneath shows through on top. If it is visible, then use a matching solid sheet for the lining.

▲ *A bedspread made from sheets is an easy, inexpensive way to give your room a fresh, coordinated look.*

▲ *Transform an old damask tablecloth into a striking bedcover by painting the design with acrylic paint.*

Painted Damask Spread

It is easy to transform an old damask tablecloth into an exquisite bedcover by painting in the floral or geometric designs already woven into the damask. Before you begin painting, look at your piece of damask and decide which elements of the pattern should be painted. Often the best effect is achieved when only the central or oval portion of the cloth is painted. Damask with floral designs lends itself to soft pastels; damask with geometric designs comes to life with Art Deco colors like pink, gray, and maroon.

If the design you have selected to paint on your damask is difficult to see, mark the edges of the design with a pencil or light-colored basting thread. It would be wise to practice your painting technique on a damask napkin before tackling the spread.

Choose up to four colors of acrylic paint to paint your design. You will also need one tube of white acrylic to make pastels. Mix the acrylic paints with water. Use mostly water and only a drop of paint, mixing until the solution is the consistency of opaque water. Stir the paint each time the paintbrush is dipped. Dip the brush into the paint solution; wipe excess paint off the brush. Start painting in the center of each flower or leaf. Lightly brush the fabric in the direction of the threads. (Note: The fabric will soak up any moisture in the brush. Since the color moisture will seep across the fabric, do not paint to the edge of the pattern.)

Let the paint dry thoroughly. Once the color is dry, it is permanent. You may gently hand wash your cloth, but do not dry-clean it.

To make coordinating sheets, trace selected designs onto tracing paper with a soft lead pencil. Place the sheets over the tracing paper (the design will show through the fabric) and trace the design onto the sheets with a pencil. Paint the designs on the sheets, using the instructions given above.

Folding Screens

Folding floor screens are large enough to have considerable impact in decorating, and they also serve to hide unsightly vents or cracks, create extra storage space, or make the proportions of a room seem more comfortable. Small folding screens make excellent covers for fireplace openings in warm months.

Finding the right screen for your needs can be difficult and expensive. But with some simple carpentry skills and a little ingenuity, you can make your own from plywood panels and wallpaper.

Begin by choosing a good grade of ¾-inch plywood to prevent warping. For panels up to 15 inches wide, AC grade plywood works well. But for wider panels, which are more likely to warp, it is a good idea to use the more expensive cabinet grade of birch veneer plywood. Be sure to choose wood with few surface blemishes.

The height of the screen should be in proportion to the height of the room. With an 8-foot ceiling, use a screen that is no more than 6 feet tall.

The width of the screen panels may vary according to the pattern of the wallpaper you use to cover them. For example, you can cut three 16-inch-wide

▲ *A small fireplace screen, covered with wallpaper, contributes a colorful accent to the room.*

panels from a single 48-inch-wide sheet of plywood. But if the repeat of your wallpaper is wider than 16 inches, you will need to cut wider panels.

Often the store where you purchase the lumber will cut the plywood into panels at little or no cost. But for more complicated cuts, take the wood to a cabinet shop.

To prepare the wood, fill in the cut edges of the panels and any surface blemishes with wood filler. Allow the wood to dry; then sand. Repeat if necessary to achieve a smooth surface.

To seal the wood, paint both sides and all edges of each panel with a coat of oil-base primer. Then paint the back and edges of each panel with one or two coats of oil-base paint. Use a color that coordinates with the background of the wallpaper that will cover the front of the screen.

Mark one edge of the first panel for placement of the hinges. Lay the panel flat and position the top and bottom hinges at least 1 inch from the ends of the panel. For smaller screens, two hinges per panel joint will be enough. For larger screens, center a third hinge between the top and bottom hinges.

Using a pencil, mark the locations of the screws on the side of the panel. Remove the hinges and drill the holes for the screws with a hand drill or a power drill, using a drill bit slightly smaller than the diameter of the screw. Replace the hinges and attach them with screws.

Close the hinges and lay the second panel over the first panel, matching the edges. Open the hinges and mark the placement on the second panel. Drill holes for the screws and attach the panel. Repeat to join the remaining panel.

Carefully measure and cut lengths of wallpaper to cover the fronts of the panels. Using a brush or roller, apply wallpaper paste to the back of the paper. Stand the screen up and apply the wallpaper to the panels. Wipe off any excess paste with a damp sponge. Trim the paper flush with the edges of the panels. Allow the paper to dry.

Trim the screen with wallpaper borders or use glue to apply braid or other trims. Cut a ¾-inch-wide strip of felt and glue it to the bottom edge of the screen to protect the floor.

▲ Wallpaper borders applied at the top and bottom and at chair rail height give a screen a paneled effect.

Painted Cutouts

If you like the look of porcelain but prefer a more lighthearted approach, consider oversize painted cutouts. Stencil the cutouts with designs borrowed from authentic Chinese vases and bowls for an inexpensive way to add a burst of color to any room. The cutouts are not complicated to make, so you can acquire an impressive collection in no time at all.

Pretend porcelains look great when grouped together. During the summer, mass them in front of an empty fireplace, overlapping the pieces slightly to create an illusion of depth.

Break up the collection when cool weather arrives and create a formally balanced arrangement of four or five pieces on the dining room buffet or sideboard. Or cluster two or three at the base of a table in an entrance hall.

When decorating with these cutouts, remember that they are made to be viewed head on. The easel-type stand that is glued to the back of each piece will show from any other angle.

To make the cutouts, draw a pattern for each shape desired on heavy paper. Trace the patterns on ⅛-inch-thick pressed board and cut out with a hand-held jigsaw or saber saw. (If you prefer, you can have a cabinet shop do this part of the work for you.) Cut elongated triangles from the scrap pressed board to make easel-type stands.

Paint the front and back of each piece with an oil-base primer. Allow the paint to dry, then sand. Paint each piece with blue or white oil-base enamel.

While the pieces are drying, you can cut your stencils. (Instructions for making your own stencils are in the section on stenciling walls.)

Plan the placement of the stencils by tracing the designs onto the paper pattern. Then stencil the design onto the pressed board, using acrylic paints and a stencil brush. Since the design and the background are painted in highly contrasting colors, it may take two light coats of paint in the stenciled area to get full, even coverage. Touch up any mistakes with a small paintbrush.

▲ *Grouped together, the cutouts provide a versatile alternative to a fire screen in summer.*

Cut a second stencil to paint the center of the flowers or the scales of the fish, or you may prefer to paint the details freehand.

Allow the cutouts to dry thoroughly; then seal them with a coat of clear varnish to protect the designs and to allow for easy cleaning. Use a hot-glue gun to attach the easel stand to the back of each piece.

Table Lamps

Making a lamp is an economical way to add a new look to any room. The materials are easily found at most hardware stores and lamp shops, but the fun is deciding on an interesting base.

Any clay pot can be turned into a lamp by inverting the pot and using the drain hole for the harp and wires. The pot can rest on the electric cord since pot edges are not sharp.

An inexpensive glass hurricane shade also makes a suitable lamp. Fit the shade with a wooden base (found at most lamp shops) and fill it with a collection of buttons, matchbooks, seashells, small pine cones, or even coffee beans. You may choose to leave the lamp parts showing for a more contemporary look.

With a little imagination and the addition of a pretty shade, a sturdy basket can be transformed into a lovely lamp. For an elegant touch, add a black, pleated shade to the basket lamp.

To make the lamp, assemble all the parts (except the wire and socket) in the order indicated in the diagram. Begin inside the base; work upward, adding one part at a time. Add the wire and socket last. Loosen the two screws on each side of the socket and wrap an exposed end of the wire around the stem of each.

▲ *An inverted clay strawberry pot is an innovative base for a make-it-yourself lamp.*

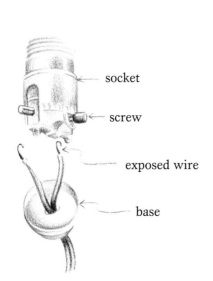

- socket
- screw
- exposed wire
- base

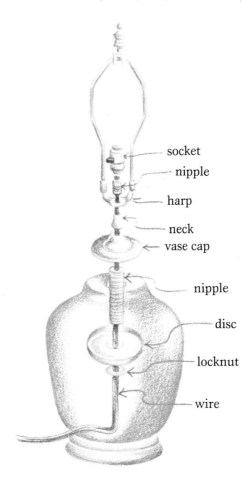

- socket
- nipple
- harp
- neck
- vase cap
- nipple
- disc
- locknut
- wire

205

Photographer & Designer Credits

Note: Photographers' names appear in italics.

Jacket photograph
  Colleen Duffley
Page 2
  John O'Hagan
    designer: Julia Hamilton Thomason
Page 8
  John Rogers
    stylist: Bonnie Warren
    designer: Ann Brown
Page 10
  Cheryl Sales
    designer: Richard Tubb
Page 11
  Bill Stites
    stylist: Joetta Moulden
Page 13
  left: *Beth Maynor*
  right: *John O'Hagan*
Page 14
  Bill Stites
    stylist: Joetta Moulden
Page 16
  John O'Hagan
    designer: Tim Brown
Page 17
  John O'Hagan
    designer: Tim Brown
Page 18
  John O'Hagan
    designer: Tim Brown
Page 19
  John O'Hagan
    designer: Tim Brown

Page 20
  Bill Stites
    stylist: Joetta Moulden
    designer: Anna Wood
Page 21
  Bill Stites
    stylist: Joetta Moulden
    designer: Anna Wood
Page 22
  John Rogers
    stylist: Bonnie Warren
Page 23
  John Rogers
    stylist: Bonnie Warren
Page 24
  John O'Hagan
    designer: Betsy Brown
Page 25
  Cheryl Sales
    designer: Richard Tubb
Page 27
  Cheryl Sales
    designer: Richard Tubb
Page 28
  top left: *Ardon Armstrong*
  top right: *John O'Hagan*
    designer: Ann Best
  bottom: *Mike Moreland*
    stylist: Ruth Reiter
    designer: Elizabeth Potts
Page 29
  John O'Hagan
    designer: Betsy Brown

Page 30
Bill Stites
 stylist: Joetta Moulden
Page 31
Sylvia Martin
Page 33
William Bennett Seitz
 stylist: Joanna Seitz
Page 34
William Bennett Seitz
 stylist: Joanna Seitz
Page 35
William Bennett Seitz
 stylist: Joanna Seitz
Page 36
Beth Maynor
 stylist: Tynette Cerniglia
Page 37
James Levin
 designer: John De Santis
Page 38
Gary Parker
 designer: Julia Hamilton Thomason
 rug design: Pat Horton
Page 39
Gary Parker
 designer: Julia Hamilton Thomason
 rug design: Pat Horton
Page 40
William Bennett Seitz
 designer: John Hunter
Page 41
Mac Jamieson
 designers: Sarah Jones Nelson
 & Kate McCarty
Page 42
John O'Hagan
Page 44
Beth Maynor
Page 45
Beth Maynor
Page 46
 top left: *Bob Lancaster*
  designer: Karen Campbell
  stencil design: Mary Beth Epperson
 bottom right: *John O'Hagan*
  designer: Mary Jane Mince
 bottom left: *Bob Lancaster*
  designer: Karen Campbell
  stencil design: Mary Beth Epperson
Page 47
 top left: *Beth Maynor*
  stencil design: Julia Hamilton Thomason
 top & bottom right: *Stephen Cridland*
  stylist: Sharon Oliger
  designer: Sandra Lindsay, ASID, for the
  ASID Seattle Symphony Showhouse
Page 48
 top left: *Bob Lancaster*
  stencil design: Mary Beth Epperson

top right: *Chuck Ashley*
 stencil design: Julia Salles Haas
bottom right: stylist: Connie Formby
bottom left: *Chuck Ashley*
 stencil design: Julia Salles Haas
Page 49
 top left: *Beth Maynor*
  stencil design: Veva Crozer
 right: *Keith Scott Morton*
  stencil design: Wanda Moore
 bottom left: *John O'Hagan*
  designer: Julia Hamilton Thomason
Page 50
Bill Stites
 stylist: Joetta Moulden
 designer: Cynthia Stone
Page 52
Hal Lott
 stylist: Joetta Moulden
 designer: Salle Carroll Davis
Page 53
D. Randolph Foulds
 stylist: Estelle Guralnick
 designer: Susan Acton
Page 54
James Levin
Page 55
James Levin
Page 56
John O'Hagan
 designer: Betsy Brown
 kitchen design: Clifton H. Seeds
Page 57
Sylvia Martin
Page 58
Chuck Ashley
 stylist: Helen Heitkamp
Page 60
 top: *Akira Suwa*
  stylist: Georganne Taylor Mears
 bottom right: *Jim Bathie*
  place mat design: Sandra Lounsbury Foose
 bottom left: *Beth Maynor*
Page 61
 top left: *Chuck Ashley*
  stylist: Helen Heitkamp
 bottom right: *Stephen Fridge*
  stylist: Helen Heitkamp
 bottom left: *Chuck Ashley*
  stylist: Helen Heitkamp
Page 62
 top: *Bill Stites*
  stylist: Joetta Moulden
  designer: Cynthia Stone
 bottom: *Bob Lancaster*
  designer: Shelley Stewart
Page 63
John Rogers
 stylist: Bonnie Warren

Page 64
 top: *Bill Stites*
  stylist: Joetta Moulden
  designer: Val Glitsch
 bottom right: © *Dennis J. Bettencourt*
  stylist: Sharon Oliger
 bottom left: *Gene Johnson*
  stylist: Nancy Ingram
  designer: Susan Swanson
  architect: John G. Arnold, Jr., AIA
Page 65
 top: *Stephen Cridland*
 bottom right: *John O'Hagan*
 bottom left: *Stephen Cridland*
  stylist: Barbara Mundall
  designer: Valerie Harrington
Page 66
 Jessie Walker
  designer: Ed Hillner
Page 68
 Gary Clark
Page 70
 John O'Hagan
Page 71
 Bill Stites
  stylist: Joetta Moulden
  designer: Cynthia Stone
Page 72
 Sylvia Martin
  designer: Carter W. Kay
Page 73
 top: *Cheryl Sales*
  designer: Richard Tubb
 bottom: *Hal Lott*
  stylist: Joetta Moulden
Page 74
 top right: *John O'Hagan*
 bottom: *Kim Brun Studios, Inc.*
  architect: Marc Tarasuck, AIA
Page 75
 top: *Bob Lancaster*
 bottom right & left: *John O'Hagan*
Page 76
 Bob Lancaster
  stylist: Tynette Cerniglia
  designer: Peggy Hesse
Page 77
 Bob Lancaster
  stylist: Tynette Cerniglia
  designer: Peggy Hesse
Page 78
 Gary Clark
  stylist: Tynette Cerniglia
Page 79
 Gary Clark
  stylist: Tynette Cerniglia
Page 80
 John O'Hagan
  designer: Tim Brown

Page 81
 John O'Hagan
  designer: Tim Brown
Page 82
 Bill Stites
  stylist: Joetta Moulden
  designer: Michael Parten
Page 83
 Gary Clark
Page 84
 Bill Stites
  stylist: Joetta Moulden
  designer: Janice Barker
Page 86
 William Bennett Seitz
  designer: Joe Ruggiero
Page 88
 William Bennett Seitz
  designer: Joe Ruggiero
Page 89
 Hal Lott
  stylist: Joetta Moulden
Page 90
 Kim Brun Studios, Inc.
  stylist: Sharon Owen Haven
Page 91
 Kim Brun Studios, Inc.
  stylist: Sharon Owen Haven
Page 92
 Mac Jamieson
  designer: Helen Paul
Page 93
 Mac Jamieson
  designer: Helen Paul
Page 94
 Bill Stites
  stylist: Joetta Moulden
  designer: Karen Hudson
Page 96
 Bill Stites
  stylist: Joetta Moulden
  architect: Val Glitsch, AIA
Page 97
 top: *Mary-Gray Hunter*
  designer: Kathy Darby for the 1987 Alabama
  Symphony Decorators' Show House
 bottom: *James Levin*
  designer: John De Santis
Page 98
 John O'Hagan
  designer: Ann Best
Page 99
 John O'Hagan
  designer: Ann Best
Page 100
 John O'Hagan
  designer: Charles Faudree
  architect: John Brooks Walton

Page 102
William Bennett Seitz
    designer: John Hunter
Page 103
Bill Stites
    stylist: Joetta Moulden
Page 104
Allen Holm
    designer: Thomas Hill Cook
    for Armstrong World Industries
    table runner design: Ann McKelvey-Dryden
    for Santa Fe Yarns
Page 105
Bill Stites
    stylist: Joetta Moulden
    designer: Ann Maloney
Page 106
top left: *John Rogers*
    stylist: Bonnie Warren
    designer: Ann Brown
bottom right: *Mac Jamieson*
bottom left: *Beth Maynor*
    stylists: Mary Catherine Crowe
    & Marjorie H. Johnston
    cutout design: Susan Thuston
Page 107
top left: *Colleen Duffley*
top right: *Beth Maynor*
    stylists & fire screen design:
    Mary Catherine Crowe
    & Marjorie H. Johnston
bottom right: *Louis Joyner*
bottom left: *John O'Hagan*
Page 108
Beth Maynor
Page 110
Beth Maynor
Page 111
Turner Browne
Page 112
Bill Stites
    stylist: Joetta Moulden
    designer: Helen Dickson Davis
Page 113
top: *Bill Stites*
    stylist: Joetta Moulden
    designer: Ann Eischen
bottom: *Bill Stites*
    stylist: Joetta Moulden
    designer: Meg Rice
Page 114
top: *John Nation*
    stylist: Florence Olsen
bottom: *Michael McCormick*
    stylist: Joetta Moulden
    designer: Carol Leverett
Page 115
left: *Bill Stites*
    stylist: Joetta Moulden

Page 116
John O'Hagan
Page 117
top: *Beth Maynor*
bottom: *David Papazian*
    stylist: Barbara Mundall
Page 118
Mary-Gray Hunter
    designer: Kathy Darby for the 1987 Alabama
    Symphony Decorators' Show House
Page 120
Sylvia Martin
Page 121
John O'Hagan
Page 122
William Bennett Seitz
Page 123
Turner Browne
    stylist: Tynette Cerniglia
Page 124
Beth Maynor
Page 125
Beth Maynor
    designer: Grace Carter
Page 126
Keith Scott Morton
    designer: John De Santis
    afghan design: Pat Horton
Page 127
Keith Scott Morton
    designer: John De Santis
Page 128
James Levin
Page 129
top: *Gary Clark*
bottom: *Gary Clark*
    designers: Richard Tubb & Greg Mewbourne
Page 130
John O'Hagan
    designer: Julia Hamilton Thomason
Page 131
Beth Maynor
    stylist: Connie Formby
    designer: Veva Crozer
Page 132
top left: *Beth Maynor*
bottom: *Bill Stites*
    stylist: Joetta Moulden
Page 133
Beth Maynor
Page 134
Bill Stites
    stylist: Joetta Moulden
Page 136
left: designer: Marcia P. Taylor,
associate member ASID

Page 136
  right: *Cheryl Sales*
    designer: Maurine McLaughlin-Abney
    for the 1987 Alabama Symphony
    Decorators' Show House
Page 137
  Hal Lott
    stylist: Joetta Moulden
Page 138
  Hal Lott
    stylist: Joetta Moulden
Page 139
  top left & right: *Mac Jamieson*
    designers: Susan Justice & Jane Hodges
  bottom: *Hal Lott*
    stylist: Joetta Moulden
Page 140
  Stephen Cridland
    stylist: Sharon Oliger
    trompe l'oeil design: Lari Scott
    for the ASID Seattle Symphony Showhouse
Page 141
  top left: *Gene Johnson*
    stylist: Nancy Ingram
    trompe l'oeil design: Linda Rayburn
  right: *Beth Maynor*
  bottom left: *Beth Maynor*
    trompe l'oeil design: Sandy Zeigler
Page 142
  left: *Louis Joyner*
    designer: Michelle B. Babcock
  top & bottom right: *Ralph Bogertman*
    stylist: Alexandra Eames
    designer: Patricia Healing
Page 143
  D. Randolph Foulds
    stylist: Estelle Guralnick
Page 144
  Bill Stites
    stylist: Joetta Moulden
    designer: Salle Carroll Davis
Page 145
  Bill Stites
    stylist: Joetta Moulden
    designer: Salle Carroll Davis
Page 146
  John O'Hagan
Page 147
  top: *Beth Maynor*
    stylist: Tynette Cerniglia
  bottom: *Ralph Anderson*
Page 148
  left: *Bill Stites*
    stylist: Joetta Moulden
    designer: Michael Parten
  top right: *John O'Hagan*
    designer: Susan Withers
  bottom right: *Sylvia Martin*
    designer: Kim Lowndes

Page 149
  top: *Sylvia Martin*
    designer: Kim Lowndes
  bottom: *Sylvia Martin*
    stylist: Tynette Cerniglia
    designer: Kim Lowndes
Page 150
  John Rogers
    stylist: Bonnie Warren
    designer: Ann Brown
Page 151
  John O'Hagan
Page 152
  top: *Bill Stites*
    stylist: Joetta Moulden
  bottom: stylist: Tynette Cerniglia
Page 153
  top left: *Mac Jamieson*
  right: *Beth Maynor*
    stylist: Norman Kent Johnson
  bottom left: stylist: Tynette Cerniglia
Page 154
  top left: *John O'Hagan*
  bottom: *John O'Hagan*
Page 155
  Mary-Gray Hunter
    designer: Kathy Darby for the 1987 Alabama
    Symphony Decorators' Show House
Page 156
  top left & right: *Cheryl Sales*
    designers: Pandy Agnew
    & Violet Lanier Howell for the 1987 Alabama
    Symphony Decorators' Show House
  bottom right: *John O'Hagan*
    designer: Ann Best
  bottom left: *Hal Lott*
    stylist: Joetta Moulden
Page 157
  top left: *Louis Joyner*
  top right: *Beth Maynor*
  bottom: *Ralph Anderson*
    stylist: Shelley Stewart
Page 158
  John O'Hagan
Page 160
  Ralph Bogertman
    stylist: Alexandra Eames
    designer: Patricia Healing
Page 162
  top left & right: *Ralph Bogertman*
  center right: *Ralph Bogertman*
  center left: *John O'Hagan*
    designers: Janet Johnson, ASID,
    & Judy McCook, ASID, for ASID Design
    Showhouse, Raleigh, North Carolina
  bottom: *Ralph Bogertman*

Page 163
Beth Maynor
      stencil design: Julia Hamilton Thomason
Page 164
John O'Hagan
      designer: Mary Jane Mince
Page 165
John O'Hagan
      designer: Mary Jane Mince
Page 166
John O'Hagan
      designer: Betsy Brown
Page 167
John O'Hagan
      designer: Tim Brown
Page 168
Hal Lott
      stylist: Joetta Moulden
Page 169
Hal Lott
      stylist: Joetta Moulden
Page 170
Hal Lott
      stylist: Joetta Moulden
Page 171
Gary Clark
      stylist: Tynette Cerniglia
Page 172
John O'Hagan
      designer: Sue Selby
Page 173
Sylvia Martin
      designer: Pat Plaxico
Page 174
Beth Maynor
      stylist: Connie Formby
Page 175
John O'Hagan
Page 176
left: *Beth Maynor*
right: *Gary Clark*
Page 177
John O'Hagan
Page 178
Gary Parker
      rug design: Pat Horton
Page 179
Sylvia Martin
      designer: Carter W. Kay
Page 180
Gary Clark
      designer: Barbara Ball
Page 181
Gary Clark
      designer: Barbara Ball
Page 182
Beth Maynor
Page 183
Beth Maynor

Page 184
John O'Hagan
      designer: Julia Hamilton Thomason
Page 189
Beth Maynor
      stylist: Connie Formby
Page 192
Cheryl Sales
      designers: Pandy Agnew
      & Violet Lanier Howell for the 1987 Alabama
      Symphony Decorators' Show House
Page 194
Bill Stites
Page 195
Ralph Anderson
      stylist: Shelley Stewart
Page 196
Ralph Anderson
      stylist: Shelley Stewart
Page 197
Cheryl Sales
      designers: Pandy Agnew
      & Violet Lanier Howell for the 1987 Alabama
      Symphony Decorators' Show House
Page 198
John O'Hagan
      designer: Julia Hamilton Thomason
Page 199
John O'Hagan
      designer: Julia Hamilton Thomason
Page 200
John O'Hagan
      designer: Julia Hamilton Thomason
Page 201
Beth Maynor
      stylist: Connie Formby
      designer: Veva Crozer
Page 202
Beth Maynor
      stylists & fire screen design:
      Mary Catherine Crowe
      & Marjorie H. Johnston
Page 203
Beth Maynor
      stylists & folding screen design:
      Mary Catherine Crowe
      & Marjorie H. Johnston
Page 204
Beth Maynor
      stylists: Mary Catherine Crowe
      & Marjorie H. Johnston
      cutout design: Susan Thuston
Page 205
Jim Bathie

Index

A

Appliances, painting, 62

B

Backsplash, stenciled, 47
   instructions, 163

Bedspreads, 131
   from sheets, 130-131
      instructions, 200
   painted damask, 131
      instructions, 201

Braided edging, *instructions, 172*

C

Cabinets
   painting, 62-63
   pierced-tin, 64
      instructions, 190

Collectibles, displaying, 59-61, 91-93, 144-153, 157

Cornice, fabric-covered, 136

Crocheted rag rug, 38
   instructions, 178

Curtains
from bridge cloth, *instructions, 136*
ribbon-tied, 139

Cutouts, painted, 106
   instructions, 204

D

Draperies
   contrasting fabric drape, 138
      instructions, 138
   with bow-tied swag, 138
      instructions, 170
   with fabric knot, 137
      instructions, 168
   with pouf swag, 139
      instructions, 169

F

Faux finish, painted, 72, 173
   instructions, 179

Fire screen, 107
   painted cutouts, 106
      instructions, 204
   papered, 107
      instructions, 202-203
   stenciled, 49

Floorcloth, stenciled, 49
   instructions, 175

212

Floors, painted, 173
  checkerboard, 63
    instructions, 173
  inlay, *instructions, 173*
  pickled, *instructions, 174*

Folding screens, *instructions, 202-203*

Furniture
  bleached, *instructions, 188*
  fabric-dyed, *instructions, 186*
  hand-painted, 179
    colorful details, *instructions, 180-181*
    faux marble, *instructions, 179*
    milk paint, *instructions, 182-183*
  pickled, *instructions, 188*
  stenciled, 2, 49
    instructions, 184-185
    with varnish, *instructions, 187*

I

Instructions
  bedspread from sheets, 200
  bleaching furniture, 188
  braided edging, 172
  bridge cloth curtain, 136
  canvas window shade, 166
  colorful details, 180-181
  combing walls, 160
  contrasting fabric drape, 138
  crocheted rag rug, 178
  draperies with bow-tied swag, 170
  draperies with fabric knot, 168
  draperies with pouf swag, 169
  easy-sew swag, 171
  fabric-covered cornice, 136
  fabric-dyed furniture, 186
  fancy knotted pillows, 197
  faux marble finish, 179
  folding screens, 202-203
  furniture stenciled with varnish, 187
  milk paint, 182-183
  painted cutouts, 204
  painted damask spread, 201
  painted floor, checkerboard, 173
  painted floor, inlay, 173
  painted quilt-block pillows, 198-199
  painted sisal rug, 176
  pickled floor, 174
  pickling furniture, 188
  pierced-tin panels, 190
  round tablecloth, 191
  round tablecloth with shirred welt, 192-193
  sisal rug painted with fabric dye, 177
  sponging walls, 161

  square or rectangular tablecloth, 194
  stenciled backsplash, 163
  stenciled floorcloth, 175
  stenciled furniture, 184-187
  stenciled rag rug, 178
  stenciled shutters, see stenciled walls, 164-165
  stenciled walls, 164-165
  striating & drybrushing walls, 161
  table lamps, 205
  tied pillow covers, 195-196
  tied window shade, 167

P

Pickled furniture, 98-99
  instructions, 188

Pillows
  knotted, 156
    instructions, 197
  quilt-block, 61
    instructions, 198-199
  tied covers, 157
    instructions, 195-196

Q

Quilts, displaying, 40, 58, 61, 89, 111, 124

R

Rag rug
  crocheted, 38-39
    instructions, 178
  stenciled, 48
    instructions, 178

S

Shutters, stenciled, 41
  instructions, see stenciled walls, 164-165

Sisal rug, painted, 44
  instructions, 176
  painted with fabric dye, 116
    instructions, 177

Stenciling
  stenciled backsplash, 47
    instructions, 163
  stenciled cutouts, 106
    instructions, 204
  stenciled fire screen, 49
  stenciled floorcloth, 49
    instructions, 175
  stenciled furniture, 2, 49
    instructions, 184-187
  stenciled rag rug, 48
    instructions, 178
  stenciled shutters, 41
    instructions, see stenciled walls, 164-165
  stenciled walls, 41, 46-48, 62
    instructions, 164-165
  stenciled window frame, 48

Swag, easy-sew, 78
  instructions, 171

T

Tablecloths
  round, 22, 69, 127, 132
    instructions, 191
  square or rectangular, *instructions, 194*
  with shirred welt, 156
    instructions, 192-193

Table lamps, *instructions, 205*

Trompe l'oeil designs, 140-141

W

Wall border, fabric, 155

Walls
  combed, 142, 162
  combing, *instructions, 160*
  drybrushed, 162
  hand-painted, *instructions, 160*
  paints to use (chart), 161
  sponge-painted, 142, 162
  sponging, *instructions, 161*
  stenciled, 41, 46-48, 62
    instructions, 164-165
  striating & drybrushing, *instructions, 161*
  trompe l'oeil designs, 140-141

Windows, stenciled frame, 48

Window shades, 166
  canvas, 29
    instructions, 166
  tied, 80
    instructions, 167

Window treatments
  braided edging, *instructions, 172*
  bridge cloth curtain, *instructions, 136*
  canvas window shade, 29
    instructions, 166
  contrasting fabric drape, *instructions, 138*
  draperies with bow-tied swag, 138
    instructions, 170
  draperies with fabric knot, 137
    instructions, 168
  draperies with pouf swag, 139
    instructions, 169
  easy-sew swag, 78
    instructions, 171
  fabric-covered cornice, *instructions, 136*
  ribbon-tied curtain, 139
  stenciled shutters, 41
    instructions, see stenciled walls, 164-165
  stenciled window frame, 48
  tied window shade, 80
    instructions, 167

214

Creative Ideas
for
Decorating

Designed by
Cynthia R. Cooper

Text composed in ITC Esprit on Linotron 202 by
Akra Data, Inc.
Birmingham, Alabama

Color separations by
Capitol Engraving Company
Nashville, Tennessee

Printed & bound by
W. A. Krueger Company
New Berlin, Wisconsin

Text sheets are St. Lawrence Web Gloss by
Newton Falls Paper
Newton Falls, New York

Endleaves are James River Papan by
James River Corporation
South Hadley, Massachusetts

Cover cloth is Kingston Natural Finish by
The Holliston Mills
Kingsport, Tennessee